D0711595

TARTARUS SAUCE

(horror-love stories
spun from string theory)

Christopher E Ellington

scars publications
America

TARTARUS SAUCE

Christopher E Ellington

scarspublication

http://scars.tv

first edition
printed in the United States,
the United Kingdom, Europe and Japan

10   9   8   7   6   5   4   3   2   1

TABLE OF CONTENTS

Things die. All things die.

--Kurt Vonnegut, Jr., in *Happy Birthday, Wanda June*

This is dedicated to one familiar person known to have done The Author great evil, all the while saying to everyone they met, *"I am good. I do not harm. I am gentle. I seek peace."*

I know you well, *vanya.*

Moderator: Can you stand one more?

Johnsonia: Ohh, *ohhh-kayyy...* (audience laughter) Last one, though...yes?

Student: Now I'm sure they'll lynch me as a timewaster... Dr., my name is Egon, I'm in the masters program over at Crozer Divinity School?

Johnsonia: Uhuh. Yes, all right. I'll lend you a security guard (audience laughter) but I *am* tired. I insist this relate!

Student: It might be a nice summing up. It takes the nature of the 'dumb brute universe', the notion of unawareness, to the idea of God as not dead, but inert. If all around us, the spatial bodies, the foam of energy extending outward...if all this is purpose, but so dim as to be unaware, wholly un-*self*-aware...

Johnsonia: ...then we must eliminate anthropomorphism as a divine form? Am I correct, I've heard this conclusion twenty times.

Student: I'm not priding Mankind.

Johnsonia: Well...no one is going to lynch you, but the argument is improperly framed. If we accept "god" in the context of what I've established, "He" is the god of the deists. He created, divine force set All into motion, stepped back, and *if,* then my busy pancake merely becomes perpetual motion clockwork toy. We can go for coffee, you and I, then hit our heads up against the concrete, comparing vegetable and machines of simple, we're not gonna get anywhere.

Student: "The busy pancake", has no need of God?

Johnsonia: Nono! I'm saying, creative force is immaterial to the 'what' in our Now. If I did not simply invoke Bertrand Russell, and making general allowance for god, I throw out the anthropomorphic, on my own issues.

Student: ...these are...?

Johnsonia: That I've met too many of you. Human in full, models me, you or who, as God. And that's Old Testament deity. And Baal. And worse. Human-god, introduces "no good", because it allows personal, and personal choice. There's a "oneness" there, but not a positive one. Rather, divinity as alienated by its definition. And if we allow that, we can't call it unaware. 'That', is aware. And It would not by nature, create. 'Sure scares Hell outta *me*.

—from a recording of the Q&A period following Dr. Prescott Johnsonia's lecture, "Universe as Purpose Only", Colgate University, January 30th, 2001

Leopold's Bitter Blue Void

Three-quarters of a mile east of the city limits of Mariah's Canyon, Idaho, the county two-lane banks sharply left and inclines, deadending not five miles later at a ROAD ENDS barricade. Alert to motorists: the road is not under repair. *It really does end, there.* Mariah's Canyon began decay after the 1970's, and halted any further expansion plans...though, the road east, was halted by the County itself, because of the contents of this story.

Just as the road begins its majestic swoop and rise to short distance oblivion, a motorist has the option to divert, straight on, to drive down an old hard road which narrows fast into a paved country lane, walled on both sides by smothering wild weeds and trees of heaven, vines nonpoisonous and poisonous, festooned with many brave wildflowers defiant of Fate. The country lane appears to go on for some distance, toward conifers and other giant flora of antiquity.

No driver, though he be ignorant of the upcoming barricade or more so, know of it and stubborn, wish to forge ahead, would take this hard road, which passes into its walls of lilacs choked with milkweed and sprays of snapdragons drooping over brown, dead pampas grass. A highway sign just before the mouth of the lane, states, ROAD NARROWS. Only a compact model would take no cosmetic damage from the overgrown brush, bits of it unfriendly, and if a driver were to exit his auto at lane's mouth and walk some paces into its tunnel of greenery, he would see in well less than a minute, he'd fare no better than at the barricade. Perhaps worse, as he would see, from that vantage, no place to turn around.

There is a place to turn around, but that is all it is. A ten minute walk up the lane or careful, two minute idle by car, brings one to the empty parking lot of a former entertainment spot. It is a place once enjoyed by whole families; later, by half-grown kids in the summer and teens by night. The parking lot's max capacity is nine as platted originally, for reasons obscure. The border fence hemming the property is *faux*-Prairie rail, now in a state of collapse. There is no place to go from there, and this is not a place to go, either. The establishment, a kind of postwar family fun center employing B-movies and period arcade games, even fortunetelling, complete with confectionery-style soda fountain and prizes to be won at games of chance or skill, closed in 1984. Rather, the last report of anyone going there, much less spending a quarter, was in the year 1984. It would be a reliable statement, to those living anywhere near Mariah's Canyon, to assert no one went there, later.

The owner, a German immigrant, registered the business as "The Bitter Blue Void", but most people didn't know what to do with a word a bit too Roswell, because that made it a bit not-Sunday School, no matter what passed for hep. In the tradition of American proprietorship being a personal thing, the sacred rights of property, ownership, achievement, the mouthful stuck for a long time, unless your morals were questionable, your virtue doubtful and you had the youth to prove it. Then, it was just "The Blue". Young boys were keen to ask about the "void"-part, but no one is ever recorded as questioning the negative stroke of "bitter". Perhaps, in a world where castor oil and mercurochrome were Mom's magicks, the billing of fun with an ominous or deprecating tweak, was not to be questioned. Later, it was ingrained, local color. "The Void", "The Bitter Blue". "Leopold's joint". "The German's place". 'Correct', then, being only if others understood you.

In its day, any nine cars staking the parking lot, were considered "lucky bums", or some other harmless crudity of Eisenhower's America. At that time, and until well after Nixon resigned, there were no walls of weeds and flowers to the sides of the lane. The parking lot was first come, first served. Later arrivals were expected to make their home off the road, in the grass. In those years, no one was going to complain.

The road, because of stories such as this one, stopped being traveled entirely, by anyone living in the general area. This even was years before the proprietor died. When he expired, it was uneventful, a heart attack while carrying groceries to his car. The next day, however, two SWAT units from nearby Coeur D'Alene, were sent to the Bitter Blue, to retrieve burial clothing and key personal documents. No trouble encountered, other than every one of the policemen reporting being watched while inside the building. No movements were detected, no form or figure seen. No attempt was made to locate the voyeur. That was in 1990.

Soon into the new millennium, facts of a troubling nature came to light, regarding the owner of the fun center. These facts, disheartening no matter how it turned out for the Bitter Blue, resulted in no emboldening of any person or group to continue past the ROAD NARROWS sign.

The story herein was related to the author in main, by Leinster Means, a half nephew to the owner of The Bitter Blue Void. Its veracity might be otherwise questioned, but for anyone living in or near Kootenai County. As details of the specific instance are in fine point, subjective, and as the information itself is outside normal human understanding...and as Mr. Means was adamant on the point, despite independent corroboration, the particular, internal story to come, will be related as the fiction it would be dismissed by the greater world society.

The Bitter Blue Void, was scratchbuilt by a German stonemason's son. This man, never a US citizen, was christened Leopold Erich Seyss, at the great Cathedral of Ulm, formerly one of the tallest buildings in the world, in 1913. His early years are all but unknown.

The postwar migration from Germany brought two kinds of refugees, both running from unbearable daily suffering, but also from one another. Those who found their way as far as the Great Northwest, were more the sort to hide from everyone. The vanquished, who fell short of their black vision by 988 years.

Leopold Seyss, was one of these vanquished supermen, but had come to America in 1941. No one knew the truth about his politics, until the Information Age took care of staining him, as it stains everyone, for all have sinned and come short of the glory of everyone else thinking themselves god. Leopold by his words, had been an advisor to and trainer for The Blue Division, an elite unit of Spanish volunteers sent to the Eastern Front. The SS-trained division, proven enough in fighting to be commissioned a medal of its own, were Generalissimo Franco's one hunk of open fealty paid Hitler. The one known blood sacrifice.

This high-minded boast, was a tall tale. Leopold, never a member of the SS, turned up in the invasion of Crete in April, 1941, three months before The Blue Division was ever formed, and he was wounded on the same day, at the same site as Max Schmeling, the former world heavyweight champion. Unlike Schmeling, Leopold Seyss was never seen in a hospital, military or municipal. He was listed belatedly, in October of that year, as a deserter. Two searches for his person, alive or dead, turned up only hints.

Shortly before Pearl Harbor, in an era where border frontiers were mostly unguarded as they were mostly respected, Leopold, on snowshoes, walked into the United States at the panhandle tip of Idaho. He lived unbothered as an expatriate, until his death. He claimed citizenship, from 1955, on, but any documentation are forgeries. Leopold Seyss was never a citizen of any country but Germany. He was simply intelligent, given to thorough introspection. He had looked at the coming World War, and figured his side would lose. Given either outcome, he did not bother to change his name. In triumph, unsmiling *kamerades* would find him, no matter, and if an Allied victory, well…in his mind, it is possible anything prior to US involvement, did not "count". No one would care, surely. Others cared, of course, some a great deal, but Leopold was no longer here, and so never knew it.

He settled in the eastern woods, far past the limits of Mariah's Canyon, a place townsfolk warned as still harboring "hellers"...these would be the demons and principalities of Christendom's Bible, in fact not spirit beings, but fleshly. By accounts, such creatures lived long, extended lives on our planet, until slowly eradicated, region by region, via this cleansing or that revolution or gradual encounters with warring villagers. Leopold ignored their good advice, probably thinking Americans had no idea what Hell really could be. Over the next 3 years, he built his home. In like with the thankless work of Korczack Ziolkowki, who gave his own life to sculpt the warrior, Crazy Horse, from a mountain, Leopold Seyss, all through the war far from him, built his dream. He did so on war rationing and barter for more, work for hire to buttress his funds, black market gouging, all for materials needed.

His accent, clipped and Prussian, drew hostile expressions, denial of the occasional service. An insult or twelve. No violence, but for scratches torn on his automobile while he was getting a haircut. No serious confrontation, threatened or otherwise. The citizens of Mariah's Canyon, did not harm Leopold Seyss, agent of Adolf Hitler as every sneaking German be. They did not like it when he came to town, which was weekly, and were glad to see him leave. Leopold was a polite man, courteous and receptive to courtesy. With women, gallant in the manner of Old. Asked about the war, the Axis, Hitler, Naziism, Leopold was quick to assert Germany as doomed, its aggression, folly. In like with the locals, he had nothing humane whatever, to say about Japan. He was fair in all his dealings and made no trouble, not even about the defacing of his vehicle. These things, not necessarily an attempt to endear himself, were not why the rough, hardy folk of Mariah's Canyon, in a time of world struggle, did not lash out at a readymade scapegoat.

The reason, was where the scapegoat lived. He should not have kept coming back, week after week, as he should not have been alive to do so. The town, red, white, and all-bar fight in those years, saw Leopold being allowed to live, unharmed, as the best reason in the world, to stay its own hand.

And then, the war was over, and the Allies indeed had won, and the boys came home to go back to work. And all the "begatting", began. By 1949, the town was bursting seams, and expanding further east was voted, unanimous, by the council. Any who questioned the direction, were advised the lands were better for development, more open for growth, more easily cleared except in patches, very slightly uphill, therefore preferable in rains and winter...and that the German, Leopold, had lived there many years, already. No danger existed, or it wasn't a danger, anymore...and if it was, well, it had been sparing of Leopold Seyss, therefore he would certainly permit sparing of them.

The Bitter Blue Void opened to the public, in 1953.

This story, continuing fictionalized, dates to 1984.

Angie Brion had been up for over an hour, by the time Lorna Teague so much as showered. Angie had fixed breakfast for their husbands, tidied, showered herself (the second time in twelve hours), then performed other self-maintenance...paid a couple of bills, read the paper, called her father, changed the standing order on the milk and seen the boys off to pick up Dave's check at the police station—it was there, but he was on vacation, and the brother officer at the desk razzed they didn't deliver. All this, in an hour and perhaps five minutes more. Lorna, 22, her pal and former roomie from Fraser College, had managed to swill two cups of coffee, spilling half, suck a Virginia Slim and cough like an old woman, then shower long enough, there would be no hot water until evening. This was what Lorna could manage, in 65 minutes. Lorna could not time budget. She wasn't efficient. Lorna was good at exactly two things, and the other, was making great stirfry. The first, the vocation she plied with husband Guy in a chitty chitty rustpile of a camper driven around the US, was her speciality. Guy's, too. Their consummate skills, were why Angie and Dave had them drop through Mariah's Canyon every few months or so. Then, none wanted to say goodbye. The four-person parties enjoyed by all, had become a 3 or 4 times a year Christmas, for the Brions. This shared interest and exciting hobby, was all any expected of the others. Hikes, fishing, talk of politics, didn't rate.

At the 90-minute mark, Lorna finished *le toilette*, and by two hours, had painted on her face, put in her eyes, touched up a few fingernails overpainted to slather. She trudged into the communal bedroom of the Brions small bridal home, to dress. Lorna looked beautiful; at only 22, she should have, if but for purposes of lifestyle. There were euphemisms for it. "Sex therapists", "sexual surrogates". "Mates for rent". "Extras", "extra help". "Helpers". A rich old couple in New York, blatantly called them "toys". Neither complained. They cleaned up. Then spent it all, and more beside. The Teagues, become lowbrow and with none of the morality they'd possessed as teens, were in love with the way they lived, what they did. Themselves. At a poor 4th, one another. Dave and Angie, found them addictive. The Teagues admitted, times spent in Mariah's Canyon, were "best". "We can be 'us', one hundred per cent, with you guys," Lorna had told Angie, several times. Angie had asked her, yesterday, to move in with them. This visit, they'd all gotten out of control; today, Lorna was struggling to get in gear. All of them were ragged, but Mr. Fit Policeman, Dave. Dave, too, wanted the Teagues to move in. Angie, who found playmates Lorna and Guy a human opium den, knew the risks, or thought she did. The Teagues, were edgy. Volatile. You had to watch them. She loved the four-way marriage idea. But you couldn't stay naked all the time.

Groaning, grunting and muttering, Lorna began into the her daily labor of squeezing into pantyhose. She was comical to watch, not even sexual, but an adult cartoon. Once past knees, Lorna routinely stood for minutes on the outsides of feet planted close, with knees deeply bent outward. Squatting, wriggling, shoehorning herself into cheap, old lady dime store hose she admitted buying a size too small. The scene, vulnerable, bawdy, embarrassing, made Angie feel for her buddy, also made her want to laugh like Hell. She didn't peep. Angie, was the observer. Even in group play, she was passive, but always paying attention. Analyzing. Things like Lorna's bawdy house fish wife stuff, a ribald musical performance, affected, out there, immoral, amoral and open as air about it, excited.

The Teagues, were perfect playmates. Yet, "perfect" was an illusion; such experience of it, led to addiction, which was apparent about the Teagues, who wished very much to share their enjoyable malady. The cost was money, meals, room and board during extended romps. Gas, car repairs. They were gypsies, pretty moochers who provided a necessary service: mom and pop prostitution, networked through friends and their friends and theirs'. If you paid attention, the couple were already cold criminals, at 22 and 3...but they loved what they did. They knew no limits. Had sex been a chemical drug, both would have been six feet under before they could vote.

"I'm surprised you don't wear a girdle, too," remarked Angie.

"Huh?!"

Lorna's feathers, still damp, whipped at what might be a distant insult. Blue fire and ice flashed, went away as Angie pointed.

"Oh. Yeah. I know," she agreed. "They're fiddly. I used to dig 'em, but I'm not 18, anymore. Not in the choir, Mama's baby. They aren't my choice, but I always wear 'em."

"...because Guy likes them."

Lorna smiled without looking, a serious smile. One of purpose. Of knowing and keeping.

"Guy likes everything Old World," she answered. "Old, traditional, staid. Everything but bedroom behavior. D'you know he makes us go to church, in between stops?"

Angie grinned larger.

"He's a true Victorian."

"I know. A hypocrite, except by his standard. He's a sincere hypocrite, though. We both...we really love wh... Obsession. I know it's a problem."

Angie didn't answer. She agreed, but the Teagues were intensely enjoyed. Angie and Dave had been sweethearts since the 7th Grade. Ruts were common, for them. Any ill which crept into their bedroom, was always solved by a visit from Guy and Lorna. It reminded Angie of her mother, speaking of highway driving as maintenance: *"Blows out the cobwebs!"* A very pleasant thing...though in itself, dangerous. The Teagues, got around. Big risk of disease. The Planned Parenthood in Coeur D'Alene took care of that, but Angie often felt uneasy. She had a feeling their traveling playmates never bothered to get checked. She'd heard recently, of things which could not be cured. It portended a change.

"How long do plan on working this?" she asked.

Lorna looked everywhere, rather than at Angie. She checked herself, every curve...every pleat, and her hair. Her hose, for microscopic wrinkles. The window, and the road beyond. The bed, too absorbed by it. She answered at length, avoiding eye contact.

"*Weeeell*...we know it can't go on forever. Guy calls us 'Puff, the Magic Partners'. The rest of you will grow up by growin' outta this. Sad, sad. Inevitable. Barring injury, we won't stop. Hey. It's neither good nor bad. It's who we are. It's real joy, as long as others mind manners. It's all we want. But the money will dry up when folks get mature. Barely anyone young, *if* anyone, will continue the journey. There's a dead end, somewhere. We couldn't care. We love this."

Angie heard herself again suggesting full time communal marriage. Lorna's rue at the offer and slick grin—her turning away, granting space—was enough of an answer. Oh, well. Distant, Angie heard the boys coming in. Something about "no bets", and Leon Spinks being all done.

"We both us know, there can't be but one woman of the house," said Lorna. "Once I got knowing I was no longer a guest, I'd stop cowing."

Wide eyes, mouth popped open.

She said, "Lorna! Equal treatment, is 'cowing', to you?"

Feathers, fluffed. Words, frank.

"Ask Guy. When I'm not out of control, I'm in control."

"You're frightening," said Angie Brion, making sneaking truth an odd compliment.

"Well," said Lorna, and the voices were near, loud and Spinks was ready for the nursing home, "I can be."

"...if Ali had been immortal, there'd be no question," said Dave, as they entered without knocking. Both were immediately into more than marital duty kisses, and for a few seconds, the room began close and humid. Then, Guy peeled himself off his bride to announce they all "got to be Joe Cool and hang out at the pool hall."

Lorna's forehead scrolled, windowblind.

"What is this?"

Guy jerked a thumb at Dave.

"Webelo, here, wants to play video games."

Dave explained, "It's an old time hang out, outside town, pinball parlor, but more. Don't know if we ever mentioned it. A confectionery, you know, but there're postwar skill games, even indoor rides! The kinda joint that goes back before us. It's called, 'Leopold's'. It's a way to get out, stretch. Get some air, before we..."

He was standing far too close to Lorna's left shoulder. On the right, Guy hemmed her in closer.

Guy said, "I'm not convinced, 'out', is where we need to be, Dave. Me, I'm breathing fine. And fast."

Angie watched their grins of intent. She loved these moments, always along for the ride...usually, a fantastic one.

Lorna, with fingertips hard, pushed the wall of men apart at sternums, in full control.

"*Nooo*...rather than have pursuits droop to substandard, let's go to the funhouse and be kids. We can grow up later, and be glad."

General agreement. Dave retrieved his keys. A minute on, their Cordoba was sailing through town. The Teagues sat together, in the back.

Mariah's Canyon was small. The trip took ten minutes. It was a strange drive. Dave held up most of it. Sentences ending in question marks, got maxim-length replies. Lorna would butt in, overtalk if Guy began to speak in detail; Angie, glancing back at the wrong time, saw Guy grab Lorna's knee to silence her. The Brions both caught knowing looks between their playmates. Not sexual. Like that, but muddier.

The slow pull off the main county road and creep down the lane through dense greenery, had the Teagues absorbed, kids on an adventure, but also heightened in alert.

"Who's executing who?" asked Guy, and Angie looked at him like he was deranged.

They turned at the end, into the nine car lot. Only one automobile, hugging the far end, was present. The Brions knew it to be Leopold's. He shared it with his nephew, for jaunts into town.

The admiration for old Americana, forms of entertainment remembered, was hushed, until they parked. Then, the Teagues spilled out of the back. Guy looked like he'd swallowed a chocolate cake. Lorna was loud, and all over the lot.

"Oh, I love these old places like this!" she said, fair squealing like the girl she still was. The bad girl, but remembering when she'd been good.

"Very cool," said Guy, admiring the "old" of it. Then, "Why is it out here in the brush?"

"It was always out here, bud," Dave said. "Thirty years ago, there was no brush. It was cleared, the grass mowed..."

Lorna said, "Shut up, you're gonna make him cry for childhood, again!"

"...and the town was miles away! More, when this was built. The owner's a German. They're good at organizing things, I hear."

Gang laughter, Lorna's too loud in aide of "fun".

"I wouldn't know," said Guy, "my Dad served in the Pacific Theater."

"Awww...!" said Lorna, grabbing his arm, hugging herself to him. Angie took note. *"Keep it light." "Let everything be fun."* The Teagues were potential felons, arrested in development. A seriously decayed social intellect. The couple had become two people each, in order to never give up one.

The fun center's entrance, consisted of a pair of thick, speckled plexiglass doors with large chrome handles. All this, had been fitted perhaps ten years before. Leopold Seyss, was known to refit the entrance every so-and-so-often. The foursome, once inside, gasped or smiled or cheered, according to sense memory's effect. From claw machine to "love tester" to electro-mechanical you-name it, a fortune teller frozen in mid-spread, a quiz machine on which Angie had once set a record...domed coin hockey, with players who looked made of iron...tiny versions of rides one might find at Six Flags, in addition to a thirty foot ceiling to floor Sledcoaster. Naturally, low grade gambling winked at by the inspector—"NO REFUNDS. YOU HAVE A BRAIN.", was the disclaimer.

Guy, ever the consumer despite their gypsying, fingered a vintage pennant for the Houston Colt .45s, displayed left of the cash register. Leopold's nephew, Leinster Means, walked in and the Brions greeted him.

"Excuse me..is this for sale?" Guy asked of the redundant rare item.

"You may have to win it. Onkel would tell you," Means replied. "I'll buzz him."

"No, I only meant is it..."

The intercom, was hooked tandem with a bubblegum stereo system. *"Onkel! Business! Up front!"* blew Hell into The Beach Boys with static and a shut off squawk to boot.

Reacting, Lorna said to no one, "Holy God!"

"They're Germans, I said," Dave reminded, winking at Leinster, whose heavy foot he'd ignored more than once.

"I'm not, he is," said Means, stuffing two packs of smokes in his jacket and grabbing a milky-looking drink in fountain cup. "I'm younger than you, David. That's American. I eat sauerkraut on a Reuben, that's all."

Angie was sorry to see him go, but could tell Lorna felt the same way. That everyone had "use" to the Teagues, usually the same kind, was an aphrodisiac, indoors, but made them appear predatory, elsewhere. Angie waved Leinster out, and turned to see Leopold greeting the men.

"I think I gave your...nephew? I gave the impression I was buying," was Guy's greeting. "I'm certain I can't afford it."

"I'm certain he can't, either," piped Lorna from behind.

"It is a prize," said Leopold, all entrepreneur. "Your skill may win it, but simple dollars cannot."

"*Okay,*" Guy grinned, taken aback. He looked at Lorna, who was similarly amused by Leopold. The way the Letterman show amused, when it made fun of real people.

Dave performed introductions, and Leopold caught up with the Brions. The Teagues, on money borrowed against their "pay", threw dimes and quarters and arcane tokens into machines unfamiliar, chosen random via gawking. Losing, and quick as that, didn't seem a bother. It was after all, only money, and they could always get more. Life was cheap. The immature, emotional couple, could be frightening on a level Angie didn't like at all, but their Good Time Charlie-lifestyle, their uncare, was so free. No hangups, no jealousy in sharing each other...fun, fun. It was reckless, yeah. It was refreshing. Life was mostly drudge, without that.

Later, watching Lorna load their soft drinks with cordials from her purse, the openness lost a dot of gleam. Then, Lorna took her birth control with drama and a remark, emitting a loud *"Ahh...!"* after the pill went down. Angie could feel the liquor, but stayed sipping. Her husband and the Teagues, gulped like it was only pop. All had loosened, which meant bar behavior. It was nothing Mr. Scyss wasn't used to. Dave and Angie, here at the dear old man's arcade, should have been past it.

It occurred to Angie, in the two years since Lorna's parents had taken her out of Fraser—only to have her and Guy marry at their Northern California courthouse, then hit the road—the Brions had never socialized with the Teagues outside their home...oh, a dinner or three at liquor licensed restaurants, but loud laughter over steak and Bacardi, was natural. The Teague's level of operating, *here...* Angie thought easily of a word, but quashed it.

Later, with Seyss explaining to the men the quirks of an upright gambling pinball, the observer saw Lorna five-finger the Colt .45s pennant and two others beside, folding them, lightning, into her purse, zippering in smooth sleight of hand. "*Guy wants them,*" she mouthed. Lorna then approached Angie, took her Limeade away without invitation, poured more vodka against protest ("And I say *you will* want it."), then made Angie take a long sip, patted her on the rear and thanked her for the outing.

"People just use us," Lorna said, truthful and cold. "We use people. It's what everyone's for, I've learned that. You guys are nice, Ang'. You were always nice to me. Guy 'n me, are hard. We can damage. But we know you're good. You wash us in good. This town can use us, and we love how you love us. I had nothin' but Guy, after school. I don't...this is me. Love you, Ang', I do. You're...."

Lorna hugged her like a lover, then kissed Angie the same. A smarter ass smack in parting, at Angie's stunned expression.

"I like the way we work," she said. "You're best. I could get used to a four-way. I'll talk with Guy, tonight."

An appraising nod, lips in twist. Then, virtual prancing to rejoin the boys. Angie sipped her adult Limeade. Watched her husband, a responsible man, mature, respectful, mindful of his work, what he owed, at play with their play-mates. Guy and Lorna, wove a spell. It wouldn't work, say, if she and Dave had kids. Or were sincere churchgoers. Or ten years older, maybe. Or hard as the Teagues seemed to be.

The child trio were to the Sledcoaster, on Lorna's command. They climbed in, were drawn mechanical, high, to ceiling level at thirty feet, then shot hard, to floor. Their mindless hollering was grade school, and it was simian. Lorna, the most. They rode the thing, a one trick adrenaline dose, at least twenty times. Guy was yelling he should shoot Lorna. Lorna soon was yelling, "You should shoot me!" Angie pictured the house as filthy, an inner city commune, nauseating smells, garbage everywhere. Lorna, on the bong or sleeping. *Do it your own damned self.* Angie felt an imagined Lorna grab her by the hair. Lorna, a mind picture, hitting her, demanding money. The "talk to Guy" line, was serious; if Lorna's mind had been made, why a sudden reversal? These addictive courtesans, all beauty and pleasure and no such word as "no", had an easy mark. *We both us know, there can't be but one woman of the house.* Right, she thought. And a Cinderella. And a house boy. And your boy, who works guns and shooting into every tease.

Sledcoaster shot to floor, again. The three, banshees in their cries. Lorna's, Angie reflected, was a copy of the one emoted in the dark. Utterly the same.

"More, more, more!" Lorna called, rattling the protective bar. A school-yard fight broke out, egos, squabbling. Guy looked like he wanted to kill his wife. Looking like he wanted something.

Feral, was frightening; it drew, for the same reason. Disregard for anything but the moment. Feeding Self. Dave was a policeman, he'd won citations already. A great cover. Anything, and as they wished. Angie liked the Teagues more than feared them. Loved them as lusting, more than feared them. She did fear them. They had to leave. Tomorrow, early. She knew now, if permitted, they would stay, paying solely in flesh coin. Until the Brions were used up or until they bored. Until a moment off guard, her back to Lorna. In barely more than two years, something had happened to these "friends".

The stereo system had shut off; Angie did not know why. Lorna and Dave danced madly at room center, to Lorna's nonsense syllables. Guy, yards away, fingered the mounted gunstock of a shooting game, then looked at Dave Brion with his wife. Again, the constant threat of "turning". After five days of the unspeakable, why care about such silliness? And what, to these people, was "caring"?

"You find these friends troubling?"

Angie was startled, and not by suddenness or proximity. Leopold, had a gentle voice. No one thought him less than polished. No, it was his acumen in reading her. The German had always seen into people. Whenever pressed, he passed it off as "training". "One learns as taught," he would say.

"Yes," she answered, looking back at the Teagues and her Dave, now stumbling toward an old-style Skee Ball lane as long as any at Coney Island.

"I'm gonna beat you!" Lorna dared, seemingly high. "Ball me! Hurry up!"

"These, are children, still," Leopold observed.

"It's like a drug to them." explained Angie.

"Anything we love too much," said Leopold.

"My husband and I, love them," said Angie.

Lorna hauled back and released a roll wild of scoring. Guy cracked her on the ass, not at all playfully, before she could straighten up. Lorna shoved him back, an angry teen, before all three laughed again like hyenas.

"A child's love, is capricious," offered Leopold Seyss. "Children give and they take away. They learn giving. Through tears, as well."

"Our friends aren't much on tears," Angie assured him, watching Dave roll. Watching the Teagues watch him with delight. With hunger.

"Both, appear to have shed many tears. There are those who lose every tooth in their head, because the drill of the dentist is not worth what it fixes. Those who die in smoke, in schnapps."

"Addiction is different," said Angie, distracted. Dave was planting one on Lorna as Guy rolled. Lorna, eyes not closed but back in her head, had a "Tuesday Weld" ankle up and back, bracing one-footed.

"It is all one," insisted Leopold, a hint of the military in his tone. The kind she remembered him getting with miscreants, or boys too rambunctious.

"To not refrain from holding, because one cannot see living without. To not give up this holding, same. To not wish beyond this holding, as horrors have been, and they must be still, *ja*? It is one. A single sail against the ocean."

Lorna pushed Guy back as she went to roll, stopping to adjust her brassiere, which was wholly undone. Dave unzipped her to assist, and Lorna glanced, truly nervous, a teen caught, back to Angie and the old German. Angie twisted her face into a funhouse image of how she really felt, and Lorna was abashed for the moment. Guy, arms crossed, made comments better used at home.

The old, pretty arcade room, wasn't the place for this. Angie was sorry they had come. All of them. You had to think like Guy and Lorna, or they were singular…eventually, objects. They were at home with being objects. Angie thought of Leopold's words, "many tears." Healing as impossible, for some wanted only candy.

"They're going to be leaving town," Angie told him, knowing it would be soon—tootsweet, as soon as she sobered up. Angie needed to warn Dave against potential harm. Why a policeman's savvy did not pick this up…

"I know you and David," said Leopold, kind again. "I know you both as *kinders*, then grown. For you, I do not fear. The road leads other places."

"They wouldn't harm anyone," Angie said, hoping against the lie. Aware of her own alarm. "I agree with what you say, Mr. Seyss. They're starving for love. Or something. Something is missing. Inside them. Pieces, aren't there. They're dying from that. I think their dying is beautiful, but…"

The trio were gathering tickets, and Lorna bristled when Dave commented how few, how he should distribute them to local children. Confrontation over this triviality, was cut short by another slap from Guy, hard, to Lorna's rear. Wrestling as foreplay, began.

"A person may laugh themselves to death," said Leopold, his voice softer. Seeming to leave the subject. Then…

"They are only sad, you say," he intoned. "Do you wish them to be sad in continuing?"

"No!" Angie said, turning, upset. " I want them to be…whole."

"Und if they can never be so?" the German asked. He stood taller than she recalled, stiff, in sober formality. "Und if they would harm or injure, take thankless? If they…if disease?"

She was looking up, into eyes she knew as dark grey, but now with burgeoning violet, some sort of illusion, a trick of the light. Making his pupils large, his face, stone. A memory was there, of friends she had not had. Of people from town, who had never lived, never been in this place to never be, again. Never have been. To not exist at all.

Seyss' eyes were only dark grey.

"If they may be 'whole', or will to be, or hope beyond hope, then, for them, I pray, and to gods of ancients as well. If not..."

Angie understood significance, but not meaning. For herself, she felt need of knowing, especially, of Lorna. Who was Lorna? One, two? More? Was that "who" already, this young, a "what"? The beast, which goeth downward.

Dizziness. A swell of heat. A sea of faces, no-persons only in her mind, a human brain which employed a tiny 10% its capacity. The sea ran into itself as she turned to silly noise, party humor, laughter. The skee ball trio, flushed and drunken, walked up, were there, and her husband's arms came around her from behind. Angie felt both safe and at genuine risk. She reached back, patting Dave's cheek, smiling, buffoon, in like with the Teagues. Leopold held a quizzical expression, also affected. Unlooking, outside the linear, they understood one another.

"*Zo!*" Leopold cried, showman, ringmaster, "what now may I offer my young guests? There are many flavors of happiness, here. I lead, but as humble guide. What is next?"

Rolling eyes, Guy gave the high sign to the Brions.

"We, uh, we should probably go, Mr. Seyss," said Dave, and Angie looked at faces, off-kilter.

"Yeah!" piped Lorna, flinging hair from behind, fists "champion" in the air. *We got us a looonng night!*"

European gentility, greeted this.

"Ah, *no*...we receive so few, now, less and less to a trickle. It is lonely, more for me. Let me offer at least, a game of chance, free of charge? A refreshment, any?"

"I think we have refreshments sewn up for tonight," said Guy, his grin real but a rictus.

"Yeah, about 70 proof," said Dave Brion, ventriloquist, out of the corner of his mouth.

"Not from a bottle, Dave," said Guy, not dropping his mad leer, and Lorna was on him, hugging, calling too loud, enough the others flinched. Guy held her with one arm, and did not look at her. His face was frozen. It was Lorna's face, from earlier. Knowing and keeping. About power.

Angie looked away after catching Lorna baring teeth, veins standing out from her neck, unconnected to any anger. Perhaps anger as passion.

Guy opened his mouth to finalize refusal, and Lorna shifted her weight.

The skee ball tickets argued as spoils, fell to the ground.

"Ho *ho*!" crowed Leopold, master of ceremonies once more. "But, what is this? Prizes won, the credit of skill!"

"Oh, that's nothing, Mr. Seyss, we earned next to nothing," said Dave, speaking in honesty, but the Teagues turned as one, hostile, scandalized.

"You count these wrongly," said Seyss, squatting to retrieve all tickets, diffusing combat. "I use colors, now, in place of numbers. Not just for the prize grading. You must forget the number of tickets. It is colors, now, and—ah!"

Seyss waved a short string of blue tickets at Dave.

"You see," he said, exuding a host's proper joy at their fortune. "These in numbers, were but a point apiece. I changed everything. There are now, random prizes generated. The blues, are to be coveted. Und, five! This is for a Bonus! A Grand Blue Prize!"

Lorna, knowing only the revelation meant goods or money, danced, "Rocky", fists again upraised. Then Guy was all over her, and things not for public, were said aloud. Angie caught, "...really cleaning up off these Scouts," from Lorna, and she wanted her gone, that day.

Dave, eyes clouded, asked, "What prize did they win, Mr. Seyss?"

The German hesitated. He looked away.

"It is a lonely Monday," he said. "I am lonely. My business is too quiet. There is an overstock. It would please me to present it.

"I give everything set away, in storage."

Angie: "*Huh?!*"

"Is he on something?" said Guy.

"*Sssh!*" Lorna, an angry hand to his mouth. Guy pushed it off, disgusted.

Leopold walked some distance, to the wall by the candy case, to stand beside an immense painting the Brions had seen all their lives. The signo of the fun center. An angry, dark blue sun, a star of cold fury, the one young boys debated as "the void", always asking where it was. This painting, familiar to Canyon residents, was hung almost to floor, disguised to look like a passageway. In busier years, it inspired controversy. One brainiac, had brought star charts and hounded Mr. Seyss until thrown out. Angie, age twelve, had been there, that night.

"Do not come back, or I will show you where it is!" Leopold had barked out to the parking lot. Angie smiled, remembering all his cute tweaks in speaking.

Defaulting to childhood, they followed, obedient, though Lorna swaggered, asking how much the goods were worth.

"We'll need to go back and grab our camper," said Guy.

Dave was overcome. "Mr. Seyss, how much are you giving away?"

Angie started, seeing what she had never, before. A rubber mat, placed over the most worn stretch on the fun center's floor—the six or so feet to the wall before the dark star of angry blue. Shoes and legs never seen, ran at that wall, but, no, they did not, for this never occurred. They had not been, so it did not happen. It went away, so never was.

Leopold bowed. Grandiose again, gesticulating.

"The storage area's through there?" asked Lorna, pointing.

"It's a wall, Lornie," said Guy.

"No, it's not! It's like a scrim, in theater. Are you blind?"

"More like tissue paper, I think," suggested Dave. He admitted to himself, he'd never known of anyone to touch the star.

"*It's a scrim!*" Lorna said, louder than ever. "It's fake, yay, cool effect, and the stuff's back there. You men...you know, your mamas said you go blind."

An all around, adult laugh. Seyss did not laugh. More subdued, he indicated the blue star.

"Step through, for your Grand Blue Prize."

Guy said to Lorna, "Prob'ly just some overstock. Or kiddie crap."

"I've seen this happen, before," Dave said absently, aloud. No one heard him.

The Teagues looked about, wondering at the fun center, a vogue idea in elder form. They joined hands, which Leopold noted, nodding approval. There was in all minds present, a sense of passage. Leopold only, interpreted with clarity, as he was the seer stone for his god.

"This is exciting," Lorna said to Guy, drunken and greedy.

"No, it's not," said Guy, smirking.

"Shut up! Let something be magic, for five seconds!"

"*Zo!*" the ringmaster's voice again, but Leopold was stiff, Angie saw. Drawn tall, once more. Commanding. "Pass through for the Blue! The greatest gift!"

Lorna giggled, glancing at the old man.

She said, "This is stupid. We did nothing for this."

"That is why the bluest prize," replied Leopold Seyss, and his voice, not unkind, had dropped low. He looked at the lost child, and into her, seeing no repentance. No loyalties. Very nearly, no reason beyond taking. Useless.

"You are pure," he explained, a god-truth which told them nothing. "I can assess. You must have all there is, everything."

"As much as we can carry. Of anything," Guy said, desirous. Excited at last.

Lorna, words borne of want, cheered, "Anything, yes! We get anything and we get *everything!*"

"*Ja,*" said Leopold Seyss, irony undetected.

The Teagues laughed and ran at the painting, paper, scrim. The world was what it gave, only for them, or all they took.

They passed through.

The room, was a dirty stone enclosure, lit, piled with disused storage. Ancient, dead popcorn and candy wrappers of some years, were on the immediate ground. Ants were on the ground. The place was remote and distant, from whence they had run.

The goddess stood before them. Tall, a hard willow. A golden idol, pagan. Sentient. Something from Cecil B. De Mille. And Harryhausen. Judge, erected as by the Philistines. The Chaldeans. An armor-plated face. Magma eyes, laser lit. Mouth a perfect rectangle, robotic. Vapor, from the mouth. Sacrificial smoke.

She hated them.

She made them go away.

They had no time to react. They were two feet in the air, hands still joined. Their clothing was gone, then their hair and nails and flesh—quickly, but one layer at a time. Guy and Lorna sang horrible moans which filled the room. Moans the pitch of the most broken guttural shriek. A mutual moan, low but booming, explosive, which anyone could have heard for half a mile. The moan of the damned, as their eyes dissolved and cartilage was eaten away. They were anatomy charts of muscle and organs, without tongues, no vocal cords. They moaned despite this, as damned souls moan, from essential being.

The red muscles went away, blueish blood evaporating. Internal organs, vanishing—again, quickly, but one layer at a time. Their moan, vibrated. Strong, bold moaning squeezed from them, the hum of a power plant, but in reverse. Guy and Lorna Teague were unregenerate, and unregenerate about that. They were therefore un-generated. Generated gone.

Moaning skeletons. The goddess had not moved. Smoke gushed; if liquid, it would be called torrents. The dirty room, long walled off, was on fire without spark. The sacrifices, were on fire. Their skeletons, dissolved. Quickly, but...

The first cell of each victim, the scientific beginning of each, as zygote. These, microscopic but beheld by the goddess, alone, in the air. Side by side. The goddess, once called Venus and linked to human "love", hated with the perfect hatred described in the bedouin Testament. She made the initial cells pop, poof into squirts only divinity could see, and they were gone. Guy and Lorna, had never drawn breath upon the Earth.

...but there is one God, and if not, there is something greater than the gods, actually demigods by comparison, of Olympus. Perhaps such force is unknowable. But It alone, determines. Human essential being, its totality, is a paper which, though burned, always exists, black pepper in the wind. Those who curse God, are right: *true nonexistence, is preferable.*

The Teagues, hands forever joined, were in Hell. Hell, as Dante Alighieri theorized in epic poetry, is different places.

Lorna and Guy, were on Venus. In dense vapor and mists, as one with them, but rejected. Their spirit men drifted, hung, dropped. Crushed by the atmosphere, even as spirit. Choked, poisoned by it, strangling, though noncoporeal. Burned, charred by Sol's nearness, despite not a substance as understood. Screaming, plain and naked, now. Not moaning. Bellowing, and at one another. Blaming, hating. Consumed with all things empty. Knowing they were lost. Raging at this, spirits of lightlessness. Rebellious and emoting as volcanoes erupting bile. Bellowing. Hands joined, forever. Nothing but to suffer. They screamed universal HATE. It would never be heard or known, nor would anyone remember or care.

In the dirty enclosure walled off for her long ago, Venus drew back the smoke into her rectangular, golden metal mouth, until the room, sharply defined again, was its normal, disused state. Magma eyes, lost their laser light. They dulled. The succubus, no legend, no goddess, just a Greek heller alone among rivals, was sad. Not for the human filth napkin'd and disappeared. This, was pleasure, the singular one, a fist striking what made her miserable. Venus wished she could erase all these things. She could not, as she was not God. Something, was. She wasn't. She was alone, but for an eldering manthing. He would die, too soon. Venus would always, always be alone.

Again she faced the wall, in waiting. The goddess of Love, only hated. She hated, because there was no love.

"I am at a loss," said Leopold Seyss, smiling, bland, at the Brions. "You cannot recall why your visit? Perhaps to make an old man, feel the older, *ja?* You two, were once so tiny. Your parents, and each, led you by the hand."

Dave and Angie smiled from their fog of forgetfulness. Yes, they had always loved it here. Places of childhood and growing, were the hardest to let go. It would be nice, if life indeed summed as warm moments. Angie said this, and the German smiled, wise.

"I do not disagree," he said. "Unlike many I knew in youth, I am no prag-matist. What pragmatist builds a place for good, clean fun? The pragmatist, rears a beer *garten.*"

The three of them laughed and reminisced some more. In the end, the Brions had their fortunes told (most of it ending way off), then played vertical pinballs, losing badly. They bought "rosemary high" sodas Leopold said he had discovered tromping through what used to be Ceylon. They did these things, to make old Mr. Seyss feel useful. Make a penny. Have someone to talk with. He, like The Bitter Blue Void, was a remnant. Time, was a conveyor belt. Everything disappeared. A layer at a time.

They said goodbye too soon for Mr. Seyss, and Angie and Dave hopped into their Cordoba. Loving eyes drinking in the old fun center, local landmark, something deeply of them. They pulled away, creeping slow, through brush more and more unforgiving.

This information continues now, rejoining hard fact. As hard of fact as things alogical, can be.

It is important first, in dealing with what The Bitter Blue Void "did", to understand we speak of dimension, not time. Without deferring to cliches such as the smallness of Man or our insignificance within an expanding Chaos, it must be underscored that essential creation, some spark or nucleus past removing by any other power lesser an infinite one, is never "gone". Lorna Teague and Guy Teague never "were", as living, yet they forever existed. The distinction is thin, but crucial.

Being and also not being, is inharmonious, if not contradictory...but, it is a question of soul. Insentient, mute objects temporally owned, have no discernible soul. Thus, a hard proof of cosmic duality. A god not "God", erased any sent through the blue star picture. All other soulish, organic flesh, then reprogrammed. The Universe is too vast for a cataclysm from such disruptions. It cheapens life to admit it, but three billion erased and then, edited, knit together, all still operates. Working, without flaw. Static, nonliving things, however, occupy only space. They remain unchanged. Their reality, becomes troubling.

The Teague's possessions were in the Brion's car, in their home. The ramshackle camper, sat in their driveway. Among the detailed inventory, gold and silver, also jewels, possibly stolen or murdered for. Dave Brion, had to turn all items in to the department. As a local police officer, he knew the area where such items were stored.

Dave requested temporary assignment to "Vaulted Records", a warehouse basement full of possessions and hard copy—documents, eventually with every local and County bureaucrat's signature. Birth certificates for persons unknown, children families disavowed ever knowing of, much less having. Photo IDs with no photo. Vaulted Records, held information piled high and cabinets filled with information on human persons for whom there was no corroboration as "real". No fingerprints, no dental records. Information though, through government systems, Federal, state, local. Church, but not medical records. The documentation, voluminous, was there. These persons, had been...yet no human being knew them, not mothers, fathers, or purported twins. Dave Brion, was able to synchronize many records to time from the opening of The Bitter Blue Void. When the casefile was prepared sufficiently, he took it to his department captain, the Kootenai County Sheriff, and the Mayor's office. All, were convinced. All, told him to bury it.

"Time is killing that little pop stand," the Captain told him. "We're never going to see these unknowns, or know what to do with them. The old German, he'll pass. Then, we'll see what to do about the real problem."

What was done immediately was to halt, then ban in perpetuity, further expansion east of Mariah's Canyon. This meant the appropriate county road, as well—though, local decay had set in, already. The town thinned in population, yearly. It's uncertain, how many left because of the Bitter Blue. Word of mouth, starved any remaining business. Leopold, who continued at least monthly visits to town, was only ever asked if the fun center remained open. The old man would affirm this, unbothered by any reaction. No one, harking to his war years, ever got in his way with malignant intent. Given the crime, it almost didn't make sense.

Leopold indeed passed, staring at the sky in the grocery parking lot, not ignored but unseen until too late. The SWAT teams, ready each man for his own Normandy invasion, were of course watched by Venus. From the place she preferred, waiting. A man outfitted with flamethrower, backed by two others bearing Smith and Atchisson "Thunder Lizard" MGs, triangulated the blue star "painting". The three, held the painting in line of fire, until the teams withdrew. One of the machine gunners left the force a month later. The flamethrower point man was put on desk assignment, the following year.

The rest, is Leopold and Venus, whose Greek name is Αφροδίτη. The vineyard in which paratrooper Max Schmeling reinjured his back upon landing, extended into a footpath for irrigation teams. Landing there, Leopold held off four British soldiers in an extended firefight, fleeing east. When the last pursuer went down, he made his way on foot, in a stolen jeep, underneath a lorry by night, hiding, for days uncounted. Always East. He found himself at length, in Asia Minor. By then he was weak, blood loss from two wounds. Αφροδίτη found him. Asia Minor, is the true home of every Earthly presence divine.

Αφροδίτη too, was hurt, hit by debris during an Allied bombing. Though incredibly long lived, the mortality of hellers is unremarkable—with all the things can do or accomplish, they go down with one bullet, if a marksman be true. She and Leopold, through merging supplies, stealing more...through mutual, desperate care, healed one another. It was September, by then. Αφροδίτη, arms looped under his, carried Leopold, airborne. To her limit, each day and night—first, at two miles a jaunt, then several, then ten, twenty or more, through embattled India and China. They slew many Japanese, and locals, too, as necessary. The day they crossed the Bering Strait, slipping between naval patrols timed for two weeks, Αφροδίτη lifted Leopold at water's edge in the Soviet Far East, and crashed into icy waters with him, scant yards before the Alaskan beach. More theft and kills in order to survive, brought them to British Columbia, then Idaho, to deep woods where lived her kind, nine-plus miles from Mariah's Canyon. She knew the local hellers would not accept her. If challenged, Αφροδίτη had no doubts.

A month into their encampment, nine of the locals descended near. Αφροδίτη went out to meet them, standing before the couple's rude tent. She gave no reply to their arcane tongue (though told Leopold it was understood), nor to pressing clicks, short yips, gargling hisses. She stood before the tent as shield, smoke from her mouth, magma laser eyes glowering, all night and until morning had passed. One by one, the locals withdrew, abandoning their champion—an incubus, behemoth but young, so not sure enough, Leopold was informed. Alone, he departed on foot, as the sun began its dip at midday. At the boundary drawn for their camp, harsh hand signals indicated borders. He then he cursed her as foreign and unfit. Αφροδίτη responded by beckoning him wade in. The young incubus left, angry more with himself. Or, so Αφροδίτη told Leopold.

They cleared the land and built the home which became The Bitter Blue Void. Memories are plentiful, and in print as well, of the first years it served The Canyon. Citizens man and child, marveled at the amount of work done, the effort required, even given a decade. It was of course a matter of many hands making light work; a creature of ethereal strength and capabilities, made such work easier than any seasoned union crew. Αφροδίτη had only intended a home, quiet and at peace; hiding away, as hellers did. She had not counted on the distant town moving closer, then more so, every few years. She had believed the lonely locale would prevent all but the most curious from stopping. The Bitter Blue, the creature considered a humoring of Leopold, a purpose humans seemed to require beyond mere being. It wasn't supposed to take off. Become popular. A local landmark. Always invaded. A place of sharing and the "happy" of the multitudes. In this region, it is accepted fact a person here and a person there, is all most hellers can stand.

A recheck at the Kootenai County courthouse, showed "The Bitter Blue Void", as having been an amended brand; when Seyss was granted a first license, in 1952, the name, along with sole use within county limits, was "Leopold's Blue Room". A relicensing in 1960, grants the establishment the branding, "The Bitter Blue Void". Photographs on record and in private collections dating to the mid-50's, had shown the latter name only, on a tasteful European marquee. A private meeting with Lieutenant David Brion, revealed photographs dated in an overlapping two year period, when the fun center used both. Identical pictures and marquees, verified. Only the name of the place, altered. Back and forth. As though a domestic quarrel, and struggle for control.

The significance of "bitter", becomes apparent. The "void", has been described. "Blue", now thought to be Leopold misdirecting, again claiming false association with the crack Spanish division trained to hurl themselves at the Communists, is really just the psych colloquialism for sadness or depression. Melancholy. Quiet anguish. Demigod hellers, I was told by Means, need do nothing, as they are, have, and can do or be near-anything, given a modicum of effort. This is why world mythologies are nothing but stories of gods and goddesses screwing up or acting like spoiled children. When you have it all, *are* it all, the social is impossible, and even those autistic are less easily overstimulated.

I asked Leinster Means, did he believe "Venus" was still inside the Bitter Blue. He said of course she was.

I asked why she would remain there now, with no contacts, in a still-foreign land. Means asked where was she supposed to go.

On the subject of local, woodland hellers, I was told far fewer today exist than is thought. They pose little threat—the aforementioned sortie that first month, told the locals all they needed, about the human immigrant and his immigrant succubus. Though always watching and aware, the hellers of the eastern woods stayed away. It was they who were fearful. I pressed superiority of numbers, only to have Means articulate that, even if the Aryan *ubermensch* was indeed myth and Hitlerian eugenics crackpot, we would be discussing apples and Olympian grapes. Some hellers, he said in cliche, were more equal than others.

To repeat an early statement: collectively, it is understood in Mariah's Canyon and anywhere within hiking, no one has been to The Bitter Blue Void, regardless of motivation, since six years before Leopold Seyss breathed his last. I add as qualification, none but David Brion and wife, Angela, would know whether this was true.

Leinster Means left the area, soon after relating to me these things. When asked of the current state of the Bitter Blue, he claimed he has not seen its interior, since a year after his relative's demise. After clearing every personal and necessary legal item out of the fun center, he was advised his presence was no longer wished. In years since, at peak of daylight, he admitted to on occasion driving down the narrow, single lane. Just to the end, to then turn around. Aside from any expected dilapidation, there is one change to the derelict fun center, noticed early on, remaining as altered, to date.

The Main Entrance, is in its entirety gone, no chrome handles, no plexiglass doors. There is now in place of these, since 1991, a large, bold painting of a dark blue star.

Let Me Do Whatever the-hell I Want, Forever

The cell phone was dead. SIM card removed and melted on the gas stove, instrument itself fried in the toilet then smashed to pieces with a hammer. They weren't getting their evidence that way...or tracing his movements. Guy put the grommets into his backpack, anyway. It was almost time to jet. There was no cash in the place; he'd had a thorough look, while waiting to strike.

The murderer was checking the clip in his military-issue pistol, when, entering the room where Lorna lay dead, she instead lay living. Bloodsoaked. Gasping, which brought his lightning glance. Holding home security at just the right, range-trained angle.

"*Here's mine,*" she said, and blood ran off her lolling tongue as she fired.

Guy had no equal bead on his Ex, but he got off a twisted shot when she knocked him on his back with a second bullet. This odd shot, blew open the saphenous vein in her left leg. After ten minutes of shrill, mouselike squeals and maybe a third that of flailing, Lorna Jensen bled to death on the hardwood of her own, "sitting room" floor. Guy, gutshot, lasted into the evening hours, but could not rise. No one outside the well insulated home, heard anything.

By what would have been 1:00 P.M. Greenwich Time the next day, their immortal spirits were already in an antechamber between dimensions, and dormancy was induced, an inactivity of sentience for better managing annihilation, if not revived. The spirit pair were a correlated pair, a proper match but restricted and disobedient to those restrictions. Rebellion and obstinacy over millions of milliards of aeons, violations and broken covenants, demerits and crimes against The Greater, had made this pair good only for experimentation. The spirits, their essential sparks, were preserved solely for that reason. At a fixed point into the never ending future, they would have use. They would not enjoy their use, but all essence found being desirable, opposed to nothingness.

Guy, the persona his spark most clave to, the ident of all myriads most enjoyed, saw the massive welder's glove move up and gone, through heavy clouds of purification and cell sealing. He sat up, first tiny, The Incredible Shrinking Man on a doll bed, then man as baby boy, dwarf to scale in Brobdingnag bed. Then, all proportion and scale allowed for his relative being, and he was in the long pan of storage. He slid seemingly human legs out, feet going to ground in the manner of *homo sapiens*. The storage area, deep storage, was cold, as it was space, space with an atmosphere, and Guy considered the other pans, closed as casks, internment, waiting for chances, for opportunity. Mercy. The last, was bullshit. No free lunches, not even here. You could offer or give the godhead nothing, It was entire, one, complete...but likewise, It didn't give you Christmas presents. For presents, you had to dance. Even then, occasionally the godhead shot a round at your feet.

He as totality—all the godhead's toys woke completed, before being sliced like a salami, exact for a proscribed dinner—left storage with regret. Guy's case...his and Lorna's, the utter ident she preferred...was one considered insoluble. There would be no awakening, here, ever again. They were out of chances. What burden they were handed, what prisoner's effects, what "deal", would be the last. Guy knew it would be bullshit. Lorna, neither himself, could make work what tools they were given. It had to do with limitations. The godhead, didn't seem to understand that.

He moved out into, then in, out of. "Walked", as *homo sapiens* did, the appearance, at least. Walked down, out of a labyrinth, up, into a citadel. It wasn't actual "walking". It merely wasted time, where Time as any sentient life might comprehend, was not.

He stood in a doorway, one of the aforesaid No Time, and knelt into shoes he knew were there, *faux,* painful feet. "Oh, hi, there!" was his greeting, silliness, but really sarcasm, but really masking what consumed both him and Lorna: *"Why won't you just let us be happy?"* The godhead knew what was masked. Nothing was masked. Finitude just "thought" it was, and all thoughts were found wanting, as all were finite, therefore incorrect.

Courtroom. Unneeded, fake. A falsification for reference point. It meant a chance offered, no matter how shitty. Annihilation, just happened. Sparks were not preserved to awaken for drama, other than that which they created.

The godhead, speaking from every square inch of the court, bade him greet his consort, and Guy as chosen ident, turned.

The bench, which could not have been longer than a standard church pew of 20th Century Earth, in perspective showed an aspect of miles, a trick of infinite regression, without any trick involved. Upon the endless finite bench, sat Lorna...and Lorna and Lorna and Lorna and Lorna, forever out of comprehension. Guy, from forced, inescapable, direct communion with Creator, knew the row of Lornas were representative of "all slivers". Facets of being, every. What was offered, what was accessible, what strengths, special abilities. Any combination of anything possible brought to the table of the pair bond, or offered up for community, for growth, building or development. Sacrifice.

Every formula of potential as endowed, imbued, bestowed. The First Inaccessible of Lornas, each and every, nothing ignored. Every splinter of Lorna, blinked from God's REM...not a DNA or astrological or environmental caging, either. All as altogether, comprising god, little "g", outside of Time...though as creation, of necessity, lesser—Archie Bunker's devaluing assessment of biblical Woman, was true of all creation. A boat you built, was not you. A home you built, was not you. Children birthed, were never, ever You, romanticism aside. Mere existence, was its own. All handiwork, was necessarily lesser. A "cheaper cut". The godhead did not create a rock so big It could not lift it, therefore the godhead did not create another Trinity. Math on a level with a child's blocks, spoke the "Therefore".

...which is why the bench was All Lorna Intrinsic, all permutations. The positive, the "good"...the negative, the "evil". Galaxies more encodings than some little angel on one shoulder and a little devil on the other. Every shade, every hue of angel and saint and heroine and champion. Every stench, every glop of devil and murderess and villain and inquisitor. In *homo sapiens*, throughout Time within Time, what landed was what stuck. A fixed set of points, via throw of polysided dice. Outside Time, every human spark, god-little "g", was known. Kept in quarks of sparks made dead ashes, to be activated for purpose. Things tended to skew or go awry when Man, any, was not hobbled. It was rather like keeping a serial killer in shackles.

The Lornas, star eyes all matching, waited upon Guy. He knew his Self in full extended as far behind, the same conditions, every accounting any computer system of any race could have tabulated. They were unconnected centipedes, though far more Legion, but under The Thumb. Even their understanding, and how to make chessmaster-use of it.

The judge's bench, held no one. It was symbol only, metaphor only, a "Thou Shalt Not". The coming judgement, was allowing choice for a creation experiment. The star pair, in the godhead's presence, understood it had come to this. Since before three creations prior to any explosion outward into separated spatial bodies, Guy Teague and Lorna Jensen, known by 9 billion other idents, had refused all existence arrangements, offers, bribes, conditions. They were as quintessence, unregenerate. Nothing was ever good enough. Punishments and hells and gehennas and imprisonment and tortures and re-imbuing and every illumination of mind and deeper spirit, could not make them operate as loyal to anything other than Self or their pair bond as demanded...and, surprise, creation did not "demand". Not a mustard seed, not a fig tree, not a mountain and not mouthy, bawling Man. There were, and from first minting, a few who could not be fixed or made to understand. After milliards of epochs of cosmological expansion, both through entropy and chaos, there remained a handful of reprobates. Bad seeds. The last rebels standing. For Lorna and Guy, this was Dr. Obvious material, a "leave us alone"...but, again, creation didn't get to line item. Eternity, though to Man it seem antithetical, was not a salad bar.

All of Lorna and All of Guy, were told, the explanation resounding, solid, thorough, enough their spirit forms vibrated, shaken puppets, from the words:

Choose a combination of Selves. One male, one female. In direct harmony with the choice as made, you will be placed upon an undeveloped spatial body, and become its Adam. Your fruit wrought, in another many thousands of years, will show what You as pairing, could provide or give or achieve. Our question to be answered: Can those wholly unwilling to obey or follow even that Infinite, create anything, left to their own?

Choose your pairing of symbiotic Self. You will then be removed to what balance is required for the experiment.

The courtroom disappeared. They were cramped together in a cell of black builder's stone the size of a Tiger cage, miles inside rock. In addition to the tortuous confines, it was pitch, genuine stygian; their beings, were the only light. Their thinking, outside the godhead's presence, was now limited, but both as original creation were megabrilliant, so both knew you didn't outthink the infinite computer.

"It's a trick," said Lorna.

"Yes," said Guy. "To make us slit our throats."

"I mean, there will be suffering, no matter what we choose. We are 'Adam'. There won't be any *crepe suzette*, air conditioning or porn. We'll be The Purpose-Driven First Family, and live in shit."

Guy's eyes were at the black stone, discerning.

"If it hurts from without, if that's given," he said, "then, 'impervious', is what's required. 'Shit', is relative, but if it gets heaped on us regardless of choice, then play the Big Casino.

"Choose us as completed, as gods. We want us All."

She smiled at that, and he smiled because she did. They giggled. They truly were noncompliant creations. Lorna then stopped, considered the black stone in their crushing cell. Her eyes were cold lasers. Said lasers, grew grave.

"We will require nothing, if we as realized, are everything," she told Guy.

"That's the idea," answered Guy. "We, as our All in All. What more? What need of more?"

"...but that is the point," she countered. "We will be given nothing."

"No matter choice," he said, "are we going to build anything, anyway? Knowing us and what we would choose...it'd be kind of as the old *Outer*

Limits, that miniature planet—more or less an Earth, but evil and harming. Cruelty and violence as celebrated. Sinister Earth. Raunchy, Killer Earth. Molly Hatchet album cover-Earth. Blood Earth. That'd be your vote, wouldn't it? Coal soul'd ugly black lizards of haters and perverts?"

"...and, the godhead would balance that, by giving us things. What in 'male', refuses to understand the value in being *given* things?"

"I'm talking being given the farm," Guy told her. "Does it matter if it's too hot or too cold or a cave planet or without edible food? *We will require nothing.* Not to eat, drink, strive. All but impervious to millennia of atmosphere or damaging environment. *Only we could harm one another*, so we're safe at home—right?"

She was patient. Lorna could not assail the logic, though it had a gaping flaw, hiding. A barn door. The female could not discern past the base-level equation, which was sound. Even appealing. No needs, impervious, guaranteed survival, always safe, perfect health, only selfish pursuits, flipping off their Master...they would require nothing, it was true. Though everything be taken, though they live in skins in a cave or rude lean to...though there be only procreating the new race and slowly building the first community of family...primitive, prehistoric, pre-Dawn, barren plain or tundra. They were going to be given crap, to bust their asses in a dance for forgiveness. The simplest form of said crap, wouldn't be much less enjoyable than the easiest bent to will. They would be Adam, but it would be no Eden, unless they chose Self as smiling robots, and neither one would ever, or they wouldn't be here, now. Struggle and fighting and work, straining, even for humanoids greatly evolved...hell! Except for anything *Kama Sutra*based, it would be dirty and difficult. Slavery, and with perks jackshit. The male, was correct. But. The balance for 'everything', was, preternaturally, 'nothing'. To even have or begin an experiment, what was Nothing?

A gaping hole. One through which you could see Forever's clear day. The gaping hole, was hiding. It would not reveal itself, until they had to deal with it. No danger or hardship or Thing They Did Not Want, would show itself until all was set in motion and there was no turning back.

Eyes. Lasers into masers, returned, shared. Nine billion blue, into nine billion hazel. Guy was right, Lorna would vote for darker being, if only to make it fun. Still. Perfection, to be little "g" gods? Better. Sure, Big Casino was the greatest risk. But the godhead hated them as pair bond. This would suck, regardless. Why not?

Assent. Blue sparkled. Thanks. Hazel, twinkling. In the midst of the Self-affirming light show, both told the godhead they would be human-perfect. "*We want everything of Us. Give us everything. Omit nothing."*

Strength and beauty and every absolute, burned away the Tiger cage of stone. Realization beyond knowing, other than as divine. All identity, shared, twain as one, and They were, yes, a dual, twain godhead, little "g". Human-perfect. Him and Her.

...standing upon diamond-dense solidity of dead mineral dust. Amid dead, dusty rocks scattered upon an empty planetoid. Not even a planet. With bare atmosphere. Nothing lived here, or grew. Or could be obtained as created. Or obtained any other way. The landscape, sparse rock and flat, dusty plain; its far horizon, a mottled gloom. This was their Nothing. And from it, nothing but They would live, and nothing would exist but Them. With nothing to do but the obvious.

After long survey of earth and sky, after demidivine assessment, sharing analysis in silent symbiosis, and when there was no longer any denying it, Her explained it to Him. Him no longer needed the explanation, but accepted deserving it.

"This is what I tried to tell you," Her said. "Balance, is what it is—conversely, an offsetting. Perfect balance, divine balance, and more so for experimentation. Conditions as finally, sublime."

Her continued, "We are utter and whole as human-god, one and symbiotic. We are still of great technicality, finite, yet require nothing. We were therefore given nothing. Nothing at all."

Him looked at Her, and knew. Both once more scanned the empty heavens. Both scanned the flat, dusty ground. Both scanned the grey and purple and brown dead rocks. Both scanned the empty horizon.

"Limited limitlessness. Perfection, but not," Him said, quiet.

"After the many thousands the godhead said It would wait, we may well be alive," Her said. "Perhaps not. If we are, we will by then have debilitated. This sheer nothingness of planetoid, with nothing but endless wandering, monotonous sex, and just sitting here, already fully All, will reduce even Us. If I divine it, I see us as what we once called "senior citizens", essentially in these still-perfect forms, but pitted, hobbled, stooped, scarred, in pain. Insane. Catatonic. Still beautiful gods. Technically."

"...and, despite the godhead having made Its point and had a good laugh?" Him asked, star hazels to star blues in wavelength of harmony.

Small, displeased mouth.

"I think you know," said Her. "This was the final attempt. Just being here, knowing, is fail, though still only portent of fail. Neither of Us as one or as two, can know The Divine Mind...but why It would do anything else, now, than annihilate our sparks, I couldn' tellya, bud."

The affected stupidity of a much more limited ident, made both soften. And wilt. And laugh. Then, silently, cry a little. Then smile. And stand there. Think about wandering nowhere, or sex as nothing within nothing. They stood, purposeless and void, facing eventual nonexistence without plea. Nothing on the moribund planetoid had changed. There was, occasionally, a light breeze.

Their thinking, flawless little "g", dulled and sharpened, simultaneously. One thought or movement or direction, *any*, overcame the stasis. Her turned as instructed by Him in a mutual will, slowly. Surveying other horizons, star movements, considering the imponderable of future or family upon an emptiness. This filling of mind, so disconnected already with an impossible consideration, was overload—for human-perfect, it was scant irritation of slowing and confusion. Which, was all that was necessary.

When she was at 180 in her turn, facing completely away in depth of calculation, absorbed, Him rose up fast with a stone the size of a baseball, and stove in the back of Her head. In deference to her little "g" and possible immediate recovery, Him made certain to strike hard enough, to smash Her skull, shattered, into her godlike brain.

Her barked a whine, volume that of an exploding grenade. She fell to knees, to fours, to face, then after seconds, rose as god, levitation, to knees again, still facing away from Him. Her face, was as the dopey comic, cartoon drunk, or simpleton victim of blunt force trauma. Before she died, Her even cocked her head in that fashion and contorted features in archival like.

"Awww," Her said, idiot. "Thass brill-ee-ynt, thass brllllnnt..I knew da manzz-uhd have a an-swurrr!"

Hard cough of much blood. Full body seizure as she pitched forward. Muscles contorting, a fighter attempting to stand from a knockdown. Then, a moan, as from horrible gastrointestinal pain. Then, death.

Already having discarded his primitive weapon, and once he felt he had control of the situation, Guy looked up, always the default and quite correct, when creation addressed Creator.

"I apologize for my miscalculation, seems it was quite a massive one, this time," he said. "I don't feel any lessons are possible, past the initial one learned, and being perfect upon utter desolation, worn down a hair or sliver at a time, doesn't work for me. As you see, I've destroyed, and from GO, any balance to your perfect counterbalance. If you'd like to correct this in turn, please do. I'm going to walk around the planetoid in a circle, and I'll see what you have for me, when I get back."

After an extended, crouching study of Lorna's hellzapoppin' facial expression, the young, perfect finite god walked, naked, away, toward the horizon of mottled, "Uncle Creepy" gloom. The experiment utilizing their essence, was in this wise, over. No amount of carnal pleasures nor Uber-Self as realized, was "equal" in having nothing else beside. Who woulda thunk?

In short order, even given finite perfection, Lorna's godlike corpse disintegrated, and nourished the dead minerals around her. Over decades, then a hundred years times nine, there emerged plant life, mere grasses at first, the color of goldenrod. After another century plus twelve more, flowers of ivory white and tiny bushes of a sadly poisonous fruit, appearing akin to a miniature peach, began to proliferate. By the third millennium, a colorful fairyland, a woodland the size of an oasis for perhaps a dozen persons, existed draped as a Hollywood set, facing what would logically be, given his singlemindedness, the direction of Guy's return. The fairyland was heavy with bluish mosses. Honeycomb—again, quite poisonous—had covered most of one large, golden tree, the mother seeder for its kind.

Within another five thousand years, insects of gold shell and ivory white legs, were pollinating all flora. Eventually, small, shy rodents with large blue eyes, darted, hiding in the grasses. Birds never bigger than wrens, blue and black with beaks of shining white, swooped and fought in the air. The Hollywood fairyland, by a span of twelve thousand years more, was a thick, dense forest, an unreal real, deep and wise, as from the pen of Tolkien. A brooding place of secrets. No larger animals ever emerged, and the small, quick life which proliferated, was each to its kind, territorial. Not a living thing, wished intrusion. The unwelcomeness, could be felt in the breeze. A trace of rich fruitiness, was always in the bare wind. Many varieties of edibles were available, none of them safe but for the local, primitive life forms. After a time measured by Earth men and women totaling near thirty thousand years, the garden fed through Lorna's lifesblood and DNA as "Her" stretched many miles, and in all directions. Its essential evolution was unlikely to extend further, and its acreage would soon hit an upward limit.

And Guy, alone and perfect? "Him" sat, silent, upon a crude chair of stone, quite literally on the other side of the world. Despite what he had said to the godhead, he had no plans to return, as he expected no worthwhile offer, replacement, revision or new counterbalance, to be extended. The godhead, as any creative force, had no reason to make concession or play nice. Fine, thought Guy. Screw them. They'd never liked him and Lorna, anyway.

I'll Make You Live,
I Love You So

It was nearly eighty-nine years ago. She was our waitress at Denny's. Thin. Pale. New Wave/New Age/Millennial. All gush, when told I was a writer. Lie machine, per the usual "better life" people think Others have no way of searching. She stood with us, that poor meal Thanksgiving, until the wife was cold and mother-in-law was casting red-eyed shadows. She left with regret.

She wrote her phone number on the VISA receipt.

I spent necessary Internet time; the economy was bad, and our Rent City had enough prostitution quietly going, to hark to Mad Max's Bartertown. Yes, she had, I'd learn in the future, but in main, your garden variety young, stupid girl, with hopes in 12th grade and a baby by graduation. Obsessed with fitness. Judging by pix of her at 16, I understood why. Baby Fat Deluxe, pretty and *"aww…!"* But, the baby fat of 16, made me see what had me gushing at Denny's as well, why a stranger my daughter's age had me falling into midlife clichés.

Waitress Girlie, at 16, was near beer to my First Love, at 17. I mean "close enough for scale", as modelers were given to say. And, that scared me. Badly. I had always claimed I would murder, to regain that lost ark from my beginnings, and no, that isn't drama. I just knew that about myself, had for all my life. But now, standing pat, mired in a quicksand that drinks us all, Age. Wondering about heart bets, and doubling down. And we were still a poor family at Christmas. And we went again, to Denny"s. And I found out she'd been fired.

That night, late, in a basement corner on my "Tony Soprano" phone, as I called it—I'd goofed when I'd registered, and had included no ID—I phoned. A friend, some clueless "Jenifer with one 'n'", all XX-paranoia and youth's "Fuck You". I called back and fought with her, three times. If my wife had not been a wine drunk, that would have been my Stalingrad.

Jenifer and her one-n-cylinder finally sparked, and yes, ohhh, yeah, *that* guy, the writer! Her friend, "Star", had made a huge deal of me. Spent most of a paycheck ordering my works. Lost a potential suitor over their constant presence and quoted pith (*"You want him? You want him?"*). Jenifer laughed about the obsession, told me in the candor of 21st Century Woman how sad I was "old", because her friend would…well. Apparently kill me with sex, at that point; if I'd been nearer their age, the process somehow involved only me losing my socks.

Star, my devotee, was living in poverty, worse than before, now she was unemployed. I knew the neighborhood Jenifer quoted. A drug district called "The Perimeter". The USPS refused to go near it. I expected to lose parts of my Grand Am, once I parked and walked away.

Star, oversized toddler a-cry in her arms, was joyous at sight of me. The kind of joy men say they don't like, but most do. The kind websites disparaged, and women never to be in such need, forever sniffed at. I was Star's savior. That was clear. As the Brit slang went, "I was on a promise." But I left lechery alone, that day.

I learned, through visits repeated for over a month, of her struggles, mistakes, degradations for crumbs. The dearth of family, at least any who cared. She was to the point of "anything", she told me. We all know the meaning of that abyss. The defeat of "okay…". The fearful Whatever. White slavery. Basement clubs a girl did not often survive. Being Stella to some, any lug's Stanley. Medical experiments, and no such word as 'no'.

Which, is what I'd wanted to hear.

I told Star at last, my plans. Insane plans, no surprises there. The 20-year-old and I by then were, okayokay, no point, this is clear. It was nearly March, before she made up her mind. By then, rent comp'd by me and formula for Junior, enough groceries she'd begun to take weight, never shaken from gooey, fangirl devotion to a hack like me, the dependence issue was understood. I had the say, and, Yes, Sir. My plan for our lives, basic, naïve, was the plan I'd had at 17. But, that plan had been with Lorna—"Lorna", my First. And, it had only, in 1979, involved dreams and sex and puppy dog eyes. This plan, was rather more layered. Star "got", that she was near beer-Lorna. For my plan to be realized, Star had to become Lorna. Surgeries and brainwashing, were to effect this, and her youth and conditioning, would see her through the pain.

Told you. "Insane", involves only a plan and "yes".

Anyone who thinks self worth is the prevailing issue, is a victim of postsecondary indoctrination. If you assert that the females in *Soylent Green,* for example, were trapped only by reality of their world, uhhh…YES! We're all in our own realities, aren't we? It was a "very world", for each individual person, before I could legally drink. Star had forfeited her right to manage life on her own. She knew that, and knew what any real "help", meant. Anyone who helped her reclaim control, controlled her, up to and past that point. A straight-"A" student (as had been my Lorna), she was a quick study: *If Life hands you lemons, barter them, they're all you've got.* Star was already a kind of slave to any taker, and I at least, was a cool writer who had stuff published and OMG! I was in her hovel and on her futon and I was good to her baby and good to her, I bought her food and never yelled and…

Scoff your head off. You may never have found this on a personal level, but they're out there. Both genders, all persuasions, every half-click on the human dial. The already-checkmated. "I'll be whatever you want". Me, I wanted Lorna. Still. I guess it's crystal I'm not a nice person. You'll like how this story ends.

I owned a home, but only just. Star, as stated, was beyond destitute. I was 50, no time to hash amenities with my family. I just had to go, and so did she. And not empty-handed. I thieved an unregistered firearm from a survivalist I knew; Star did likewise, from a dealer-friend. A rainy Tuesday morning, she went into the crummy, lazy, out-of-the-way branch of Metabax Bank, ironically near the old state road. All by herself. With maximum rippage. She killed eight people, altogether. The camera saw her, of course, but that person was going quickly away. Her toddler had been given to a childless friend who loved him, and we left the dead and the abandoned and the patsys and the rest of our world, behind.

The aforesaid kind of passion, uncaring of Others…cartoonish, right? *Natural Born Killers.* But, hey…stereotypes originate from more than fertile minds of serial haters. So did every archetypal image. Horace Greeley didn't create that world, kids. Star was someone starry-eyed, 1000 days before. She'd been made nothing, and a person's mind, though their spirit be broken, turns dark, there. Always. The abused child who turns abuser. This "turn" happens all the time, everywhere you look. Such fresh amorality, bonds easily with any who offer to feed it. Give it a second chance. Make it new. It's the giver or enticer, the idea man or Svengali, who isn't entirely safe. As for me, middleaged men don't need to be explained. Especially not Aspergians.

Neither of us cried about babies or wives or families laying theirs' to rest. We drove South, eventually to Mexico, then on through Latin America. Our car fell apart, in Ecuador. We had to take trains and hitchhike, to the place I'd heard of, narrowing location one rumor at a time. We were, after two exhaustive months, at last in Chile, sky high in the Andes. Ultra-incredibly high. Everything was slow motion and vertigo. Nose bleeds and headaches. Star had it far worse. I acclimated, after two weeks. When the secret medical center, no name ever offered, wheeled my young proxy into her first surgery (and for those wondering, yes, I heard German spoken by a number of people, but always from a distance away), the blood on her upper lip had become a familiar sight. It was dripping freely, as I wished her well.

We were at the mountain center, for a year. There were 17 surgeries, fitting, as I'd lost Lorna, at 17. Extensive records were kept, and images. I used to have a large holo-album of "Star Into Lorna". It was destroyed in a rage, many years ago.

From Star to my First, near beer or not, was a massive undertaking. My perception, rooted in Love's memory, had been off. The shape of the skull was Not the same, the upper musculature was vastly different. I wouldn't have cared if I'd been asked ahead of time, but I'd receive reports after work had begun, like independent contractors did to homeowners in my day. Some of the things baffled me—why it mattered, that Lorna was three inches shorter than Star, was to me of no account. Just make her look like Lorna, I mean, come on, now. By the fourth month of their work, I was screaming that at doctors, who found my attitude incomprehensible. One European (not German; the accent was Danish, I think), sat me down to try and explain the exact science of "reconstructed humanity". Meantime, they barely let her recover from one surgery to the next. It was all antiseptic enough, no real problem with infections, but Star required constant transfusions and re-transfusions. And infusions. Her bleeding from the altitude, never stopped. They used techniques both methodological and folk. They used drugs, sometimes copious amounts, to fool the body into coagulation. They used acupuncture and pressure. They used small tasers.

One night, late, an insane lightning storm had me vault standing out of bed, from sleep. Nearly tore the center to bits. I was told by a nurse in broken English, the surgeons had siphoned from lightning bolts to try and cure the problem of bleeding. It had taken the hairy thunderer, and even that was a half measure. Star's nose had no plugs for more than 8 weeks, but after that, the red was a thin trickle, again. And, FYI. I never again saw the informative nurse, after we spoke.

So, the invasive procedures did, what? Ugly-ing in order to better, or here, ugly-ing in order to prettify. They were random in their body choice order, it seemed to me, but when finished and once a specific area healed, I would often weep, as I was looking at beaches and the 1970's, at skin—somewhere, in Reality faded and wrinkled and sagging. Lorna as young and new, was emerging. And faster than the physical, Star my quick study, was becoming Lorna in mind.

The brainwashing procedures were thorough, military, based partly in books on Viet Cong procedures. Brutality was used even with the most willing subjects. Star learned immediately, that complete, enthusiastic compliance. The sold out true believer. The slave she was becoming before we'd drooled mutually at Denny's, was the one who was beaten or tortured much less. She was a fine soldier, I was told, Chilean captain of the guard clapping me on the back. Peruvian psychotherapist smiling. Prussian facilitator nodding with a bang.

To all Beavises in the peanut gallery: NO. Nothing sexual in what happened to her. My pride, played Zero Part. As I say, they were tearing apart Star to make her into Lorna, and the young physique wasn't even being allowed any recovery or healing in full. Any recreational abuse, carried too much risk. I was assured by the captain, any man complicating the surgeons' work to satisfy himself, would be summarily hanged. Star, one of the last times I can say I was talking with "her", told me it would be all right if the instructors started beating her like gangbangers, because "I feel like I've never not been in pain." Her face, her eyes, reflected this. Star was five months in, by then. Batsy with the pain. Joyous. Her face one way or another, always radiant with joy, amazing ecstasy, rapture. Near-bursting with happy.

I stopped calling her Star, halfway through the process. The doctors didn't tell me. Lorna did. The face, the final portion completed in the re-cephalic ordering, was my Love, 17 and spellbinding…but when I called her "Star", or even used the word, Lorna's 90% angel face would cloud over, and electric Hate appear in her water blues (Star had hazel eyes, btw…that was another thing I didn't notice about her). Her mouth would turn down, show lower pearlies as carnivore, threatening. I saw her hands as Lorna's, crimp into fists. The last time I called her who she'd been upon meeting, Star literally came up into a sitting position in bed, shoulders back, fists cocked back and to the side, but low. Head tilted, as a mind emptied, wondering, blank. Blonde, blue-eyed, teenaged female shaven ape. The she-ape's face was a billboard of warning: DON'T CALL ME THAT. I never did again, for more than thirty years. I knew what would happen, if I did.

Those who remade Star's mind, had to erase Star as what her mind knew, before replacing it with Lorna. There is no "remaking", no "conversion" the neat, cut/paste way churchly people prefer. It's very-United States Marine Corps, but laboratory. Star as human identity, was taken completely out of everything else which existed in Star's brain…and immediately, as the voided, violated no-person panicked, fearful, searching, ALONE, Lorna was given it. And Lorna was good, you don't mind me priding my taste. The husk without personhood, grabbed up the identity, and ate it whole.

By nine months in, I never worried and never made trouble, but for the red Kleenex always stuffed in Lorna's nostrils. She was herself; conversations silly and laughing, flirty and with contentment. There were many things which didn't match. Lorna had no reaction, was a blank on any significance of me as an eldering man. Knowledge of her family and friends extended well into the 21st Century, further muddying the age disparity. Any hint or jot of a love interest, husband, lover, NSA boyfriend, FWB, zipless fuck, anything, was gone. There was only Me. Only our "ever". It should serve no surprise I'm Old School-jealous, so once I got myself as Only Man On The Planet into my head, I knew the States would never see us, again. Probably no urban area, anywhere.

The math of Age, age as reality, had been taken from her, or reinvented in a way so illogical, a person would have to be a fool. Life had gone by, yes, many years, and she was without a day of physical change and I was exactly what I knew I was. Lorna, face glazed, frosted, oiled, smeared and caked with Happy, was oblivious to any of that. We would have a Life, as Life neared its end. For all our lives. There were many years, now the years were gone. All the decades past and spent, were as a summer spent apart. Every moment was a summer without motion. Or sense.

I pressed this hysterical contradiction, exactly once. Lorna, as a computer fed bad data, began to sputter, then was fast to confusion and a "lost" look… then, the she-ape of rage was again in the room. I pacified her with diversions you'd use on an infant, and within seconds, she was giggling, prattling about her granny (long dead) and something from The Carter Years, which for her was just that month. I let the irresolvable issue die, for a long time. I let it die, until I as a man wanted death. But one thing cogent came from her jumble, a thing terrifying far more: just before the "lost" and the ape, Lorna, sputtering about our ages as exactly alike, told me conversely when she was my age, I'd be over 150.

C'mon. She didn't make that up. Her computer, not thoroughly battened into Deep Lorna, was child-repeating something she'd overheard.

The Metabax heist, even by way of Chilean dollars, was not the price of a year of medical miracles and toil and supplies, creating new Life for a lifeless man and enough blood supplied to float a barge. To say nothing of room and board. I actually gained weight, that year. I was told before they'd ever given her Lorna's face, our finances were dead in the water. I asked how were we supposed to repay. They didn't answer. Just wheeled a doped, moaning Star back into surgery.

And Month #11, and she twirled remade, in Lorna's dresses, and Month #12, and I watched Lorna smile and laugh as they asked five hours worth of identifying questions, nonstop, genius. Month #13, resplendent in white as we packed to leave, and my high school girlfriend made from another, high kicked at my head, precision, then froze, statue, Madonna's "Vogue". A playful hiss, open-mouth. Lorna now knew every selfdefense and martial art, every

Green Beret, Navy Seal, Special Ops, CIA, Mossad, Cong, Taliban, Yakuza maneuver by rote. Her skills were praised by masters brought to observe. The actual Lorna had been able, at 17, to throw a playful, harmless high kick, slow motion. This Lorna, was 31 flavors of killer. I figured I knew the 'why' of that, but asked the heads of the center, seated in conference on my own, just before we took the slow bus to sea level.

"It was implanted in her consciousness as failsafe," a very Teutonic doctor advised. "Your sacrifice of her so we might learn on the job, buys you much, but we both know you wish her to have no other consort, and your own aging will begin to tell, soon enough. Whether Star or Lorna, she will have many years beyond you. You strike me as a man who holds life as cheap in the extreme. Lorna as made, was too much work, too precious. You cannot be allowed to throw her away. It is without question, you would murder her, rather than allow her beyond your reach, else you would not have brought Star here for such purposes. Now that the pair of you are destitute, you cannot buy her death…and you have no hope of effecting it, yourself. I dare you to try."

I was then told by another physician, the sole reason the work had been completed: it was their first total conversion. One person as reinitialized, poured into already-existing Other. They'd never done it before. Not the Full Monty. The whole adventure had been Vegas. It explained the year. And the generosity. It explained the dedication.

It further explained how then they provided for us, and how if it soured, they could quietly detach. Our villa was built three miles into sand and rock, west of the coast on an island where nothing grows, to be visited quarterly with supplies by the center's houseboat. The houseboat has not been to the now-submerged dock, in 57 years. We assume the center is still there.

What, it went bad, well, of course it went bad, in wonky ways and me in the end puking sick of Lorna and every limitation I'd been blind, deaf and paste-eating to, in youth…worse, sick of what, even given brief association, I knew to be Star as a person. As for her? Techniques drilled, including electric shock, in tandem with that channeled lightning which briefly stanched the flow of blood, had opened her consciousness—I'm ignorant, here, not a science kinda-guy, didn't major in that, but I'd guess it was that induced electric flow, coupled with Star's cult member-willingness, which allowed the effect to last as long it did.

They'd scooped Star out of the remade being, pretty thoroughly. But, there's more to identity than knowing your 'who'. There's the primal, even minus identity. Star, still doesn't grasp who she…is? Was? I can't get the tenses right, anymore. All I can offer is the litany of our time here. Tell you what happened to a jerk who wasn't satisfied banging a young, local tramp, but had to have his holy madonna. Even if it meant those dreaded "answered prayers".

The center made our fate known. It suited most of what I wanted—I'm not very social, big shock—and Lorna thought our time to be "a year" (*we're caretaking the place!*). She continued buying the "year" for more than 20, but I knew within a few months, promised trips to the nearby village or to Santiago, were pap. We stepped foot onto that dock when it was brand new and finished of hewn timbers, and we've been here ever since. I call the island where nothing grows, "Denny's".

We were allowed no way of communicating with the outside. Or it with us. In the eighty-seven years of our imprisonment, only five unauthorized boats have tried to land, so we figure the center passed word. Of the five, two had the few aboard shot by snipers; the first, only days after we arrived, took a hovering 'copter, to get them all. A third, was sunk by mortars, from the far shore. Two have landed in the past ten years. They're all dead, too. Yes, she did it. The failsafe. They tried in both cases, to rescue me. Lorna (Star?) completed every submersion, even that first week. Demolition expert, too. Lorna was perplexed by her own, destructive behavior. What doesn't recall Star, somewhere internal, is a massacre-machine.

For two decades, in our womb of sand and rock, it was the Paradise Dream. Provided for by the center, me with illusions and young skin of my choice. Lorna not Lorna, not Star and not Bitcoin to buy a vowel. It was every food I wished and all the drink, sex on the hoof as dictated, the calm of simplicity, plus all control simplicity allows. Lorna was a kind of flesh android, very Philip K. Dick, whenever I considered the "killer" in her. But for recycled lives (with hers scrambled and sunny side up), eventually, the glazed doughnut smile of "no Not pain", had me wondering if she should be sucking her thumb. We had nothing non-primal to share, and I couldn't escape her, either, I found that out. But, again, by now, you know me as a bad, uncaring man, so not in spite of but because of reprogramming, it worked. Rote action, drilled response, total obedience if I steered clear of threat, we were all her smile held in, for twenty years.

I wanted gone, of course, after less than half of that, and three miles in, I couldn't get near the beach, without her dogging my heels. I remember her saying, when I was about 65, "You're not going anywhere!", and if I hadn't known this as prison before, that comment identified the guard. Even if she didn't know who she was.

So, I began toying with the parameters of the failsafe. I made it games. Can you pick up that big boulder and carry it? Now, can you do it for twice as far? Three times? A mile?

No, I heard it if stings you twice, it takes the poison away from the first time.

It's only maybe thirty feet down; the center said they'd restored your flexibility. I'm pretty sure they said like The Six Million Dollar Man. Jump.

How far out can you swim and know you'll make it back?

Taste this for me, will you?

The homemade poison almost did it. Of course we were given nothing I could concoct, and nothing that would work on its own, but vague memories of junior chemists I'd palled with, preteen, allowed for the best shot I ever had. By that time, it had been twenty-three years. Lorna, but for crown to sole berry-brown, had not altered. I had, of course, and was increasingly dominated by her, yet still felt oddly fine, healthy, fit. But for walking, all I did was lay around. That as I aged, I grew weak, withered, dropped weight, wizened, gnarled, yet was feeling better, the proverbial "sound dollar", was mystifying. Eventually, it was just more Hell.

Lorna had a nice mouthful down before she realized her mistake, and caution to the winds, I threw away any future chance by trying to force her drinking more.

With a deft judo move, I was thrown clear. She opened her throat as she did so, though, ingrained as the *ki*. This allowed most of the rest of junior chemistry down her gullet. She choked, clawed (harming her face, badly; it took years to heal), slamming around the large villa like she was having a heart attack. Lorna cried, screaming, strangling, then fell to the kitchen tile, and I saw daylight. She lay there ten minutes or more, and her struggles grew kitten-weak. *"Why?"*, she moaned a few hundred times. I just watched her die. I'm well aware, why I didn't grab a large object or a knife. Like the old fool I am, I was enjoying undoing my folly, putting paid to every boring word or unsatisfying exchange. Leaving Lorna behind in full. Once more, ego. I wanted to savor it.

Then, black miracle, and she vomited with a vengeance. I saw her gain strength after the third heave. I was on her with a knife then, and yeah, I cut her up some, but in the end I was old and she recovered too quickly, and things were never the same afterward. *"You must be watched."* I received the official speech, that first night. The words, I know, came from the center, not a person—fact being, I wasn't with a person. Not one, not two, not an amalgam. This was a creature, a made thing, a monster. "Answered prayers", sounded way too philosophical.

It was long months, before I was entirely freed from restraints, and another year before Lorna let me out of her sight, on our little island where nothing grows...except for receiving incoming supplies. The momentary freedom was false, in this context; I didn't dare inform the boat. I had a hunch what would happen. Eight years later, it did. I just minded p's and q's, figured I'd die here, as 75 became 80 became 83. I looked as much a human nightmare, as you could imagine. My health was perfect, my senses, my wind. Lorna and I still could go all night. Blessedly, she was blind to my age. Not so blessedly, after my stint as shackled prisoner, I hated her.

The center found out about it. Neither of us told them, but remember Lorna's face. She'd thought she was on her way out for real, had no doubts she would die, and mad from it, she tore herself. She tore her face, worst of all. And as I told you, it took years for it to heal in full. Many years.

So, the houseboat had to be met by only me, supplies asked left at the dock...or, if I allowed the crew to lug the stuff, Lorna would be in another room, indisposed. On the face of it, the deception seems so bald. There was no investigation for more than eight years. By that time, Lorna was becoming, slowly, destroyed. A person who was realizing her "creaturehood". I'd never peeped, but the lightning wasn't forever, so to speak. I also had the holo-album, and we spoke often of "her year". Stupid me, I figured she had at least a piece of the truth, and that it was all right.

I had ideas of time from our satellite television (no Internet), and we were always provided with calendars. The last boat came exactly thirty-one years to the day of our landing. A doctor I'd never met, young, British, examined us, questioned us. Lorna still had identifying scars, and her lies were quickly called. In the quiet of the large dining area, in warmest tropical breeze, guards outside at fifty paces, we came clean. Lorna was agape, mortified, at all I said. A number of things I said, contained the name "Star".

The doctor and his men, after he wrote some notes in "holo-air", a tech which blew my mind, departed without word. I alone followed. All three miles to the dock. The doctor, waving the guards onto the ship, held me back.

"Your tenure as guest of the center, is ended," he told me. "There'll be no more supplies. No literature. No time devices. Your televisual service is yours, until the equipment rots from age. We have never known the pair of you, and the center will disavow all knowledge."

"Because I tried to kill her? This proves the board was right, I can't!"

"It was always known you couldn't be trusted," he said, "but, other complications we'd been concerned regarding, represent too great a danger. Security, you understand. Your Lorna is...ungainly a statement, still...she's immortal, barring murder. Clearly, you make a mess of that. Worse, you've become immortal as well."

This surreal statement, elicited a visible seizure from my old, old body.

"Are you crazy?! I'm *old! Lookatme!*"

He was sad. It appeared genuine.

"You're the soul of her perfection, as far as health itself. The only piece you're missing, is no actual, physical deterioration. Our bodies don't go bad from beer or cigars or sugar, else Olympians would be as gods, if nothing. Our flesh, ages. Lorna received a full year's reconstruction; I doubt very much she'll be dead, in ten millennia. By current medical estimates of finite perfection—as it were—and I'm awfully sorry, but you need to know…you've got another eight hundred years. Nine, perhaps."

We had mirrors. I knew what I looked like, despite feeling peak at all times. How could one add to the hideousness I saw daily? Centuries? And, where? HERE?

"You may leave if you wish, you have our blessing," the Brit doc said when I pleaded. "But, you may find it difficult to hide, once ashore (he nodded backward). Why necessitate hiding? You still have this island. You may stay. We've hidden you.

"Not to mention," he continued, "she's awfully protective of you as a man. I don't know if you're quite catching this, you seem terribly selfpossessed, but the creature we gave you, whomever and what she is, comes off as immensely devoted. I daresay you're the god of this island, she, your nymph. I can conceive your personal distress, it must be dull, and more so, now, but…my dear fellow, she's amazing to behold and loves you with a frightening power. She'll look after you. You won't have to lift a thumb."

"Nothing grows, here! We'll starve!"

"Yes, I would allow that to trouble me, but again, if you'll put this draught horse of yours to work in between her being your mare, the inconvenience will prove quite temporary. It all ties in with her immortality and your eight, nine hundred. Estimates are always being modified. You could have near a millennium."

I screamed, but I was already in telescopic site, and the doctor waved once, affected a sad tilt of the head, and went Below. I watched the houseboat leave. They'd brought a larger-than-usual shipment, I reflected. In another 20, 21 weeks, it wouldn't matter.

Nothing grows, on Denny's Island. I haven't had a bite of food or fresh water, for five-and-a-half decades. Lorna and I drink sea water; we don't taste it, anymore. Our bodies are lean and leather and dry and slackened muscle. I am many years past one hundred. Lorna has begun, tiny steps at a time, into full adulthood. If I could see past the sunned carapace of her, I'd estimate, oh, 24? She doesn't know. She doesn't really know much of anything. She knows she's not really Lorna. I still call her that. I'll be calling her that, for many centuries. I found out how to extend my life for perhaps twice as long, perhaps three, as quoted by the doctor. Lorna and I are neither one good at higher math. She took it in school, but just to parrot back. She told me, however, of "immortality". How it had rubbed off. Breathed in, more like.

All right…you know the old tales of cats stealing the breath of babies? Well, of course, one can breathe into a being as well, CPR, of course, but in other ways and for other purposes. One of our harmless fetishes over the years, was for Lorna to lie atop me, mouth to mouth, lips to lips, just barely not touching, and breathe. She did this from the start, diaphragmatically. Her breath as suggested into my own lungs, was from her deepest core. A core radically changed by science and experimentation, by drugs and surgery and lightning from God. For thirty years, Lorna had done this. In my captivity, she forced it on me. This breath, introduced finite perfection. In a more limited way, it gave me the same thing she had. Apparently, you don't get a pretty shell from it; it takes actual nip-tuck, for that. Beauty, I can affirm from experience, is only skin deep. Unless you'd assert attitudinal thinking equals The Scientific Method.

So, 57 years in the past, once back at the villa, I told her everything, and she proceeded to smash the villa to pieces. Many items which still held interest or might've helped with answers or memory, were destroyed. At the very precipice of losing all control, in a visibly vibrating rage, she held the holo-album of "Star Into Lorna", over her head. Never before or since, did my dear girl image as absolute demigoddess. Her hair swirled in slowmo (yes, it did, ethereal), about and around. Her voice came from all directions and rattled the villa's foundation.

"WHO IS THIS THING ABOUT?! WHO AM I?!"

And I said the Hell with it, I hoped she'd kill me, and Jesus, how retarded was this girl? I'd already told Star her name, what history I knew of her, how we'd met, The Plan, what the "center" was, had been about. Lorna, when I knew her, was naïve and innocent, to a degree. Years into the future, Star was streetwise, known things she shouldn't, been degraded, abused, humiliated. Dumbed down, as a result. Lorna was a born again Christian. Star was a pagan who'd murdered 8 human beings, to thieve money to become another person, because the current man using her liked that skin suit better.

"WHO IS THIS?"! the destructress thundered a second time.

"It's you, Star. The You you were born and meant to be. The center took that person away. We gave them all our money to do that. You'd murdered for that money, and women and children, knocked over a bank, stole it. You had no life and no love, you were a woman men used and threw away. I came into your life and was kind for a little while. You said you'd "be anything I wanted". What you are now, a created fantasy, was my choice. A love I'd lost long before you were born. I call you "Lorna", but that's who I had them make you into. As an aftereffect, you were imbued with immortality, they tell me. The doctor says you'll live nearly forever. As this created thing, this creature of dream and desire. But, "you"? Star, is dead. Star died long ago, she was taken out of you, wholly, and you'll never, ever reclaim her."

I can't couch it more brief, than to say she totaled a huge, comfy villa, made it into a burnt out gangland shack, left us precious little to do, though we'd had little enough, IMHO. Brought our starvation all the nearer, so I'd thought. But tiny protection remaining, from the elements. None, from insects or vermin. She began a fire in our master bed, and the house smoked for eighteen days. A grunting, snarling monster, rampaging, shadow, through it. Breaking. Smashing. Destroying. Taking away the only thing we had.

By Day 18, Lorna was on knees on the charred pile shag of the living room. Entire body, black with soot. Temporarily blind from the smoke. Choking from same but never without breath: horrible, ghastly noises that went on, hours, until she passed out. Hands broken and soaked in blood. The word "Hate", her only spoken vocab, when it could be gotten out whole, in the voice of the victim darkened through learning. The loving child abused, who sees that, no, there is no love. I told you earlier. Every harmed Good, becomes Harm as well.

Rain and wind and scuttling things, took only a few months to finish her work. Today, the villa is as any old ruin, and what lives in it, we'd rather not encounter. We spend our time rarely more than between the beach for salt refreshment, our mouths inured, and a deep groove in a nearby natural over-hang, padded with mildewed, molded, shredded, soiled, decayed bits of every cushion, pad or soft material from the villa. It's the place we stay most. Sunlight, rarely hits directly. As shaded a space as we have. Thoroughly warmed, never stifling. The occasional monsoon has us wrapped up in our dis-gusting rags together, holding on for dear life…but we do that, anyway, and have now, for fifty-five years.

For more than a year, Lorna/Star-thing spent most of her waking wander-ing the island as tortured siren, wailing and railing and crying. For help. Death. I stayed in the villa as long as I could, in lean-to's and behind battle-ments of my creations, but the food went in short order, even though Lorna stopped eating immediately, and after I'd watched us neither shrink much nor sicken at all, well into what I guessed was the second calendar year, I stopped her one day, called a truce to confer. What followed, was the resignation in which we live our hideous physical eternity.

Even young and vital without peer, Lorna by commuter standards, yes, now, is hideous. Destroyed by elements free and near-constant sun, barely ever bathing, naked for half a century, bitten through, scabbed into a carapace over the one surgeons covered Star, long hair hard against her face and neck, wrapped mermaid, dirty, around the rest of her. A kind of soot creature, from sediment and Nature's dust. Though immortal, nearly blind, this time from the sun. She carries me, now, when we chance to leave our groove. I direct her. Again, I think of Mad Max, and the champion of Thunderdome. She's Blaster, to me as Master. I am a fossil—fit and fine, healthy, my thinking ordered… but shrunken, a shriveled artifact in the mighty arms of The Monster. Lorna-thing, is mentally destroyed, but at last, tame. And needy. Again, my wish fulfilled, in a quiet, hopeless *sheol* of living death. Lorna knows only that there are Two, and that without me, there is Alone. She is pledged I will dwell with her, forever…thus, but for our salt drinks, and me weakly scrubbing as nearby she walks a post, it is the groove, warm, womblike. As I said, we're wrapped together, most often she covering me. We knit into a ball, deep, aching lovers' full embrace. Lorna holds my old face and old, old head. Our lips barely touch, but are one.

We share breath.

Her breath keeps us alive and virtually immortal.

If you were to ask am I sorry, I'd say of course, but not for what I did. If I'd not hunted up Star, that goofy, sweet waitress at Denny's, the Lorna close-enough-for-scale who was nice to a man just because he was a man, I'd have continued. In my life. Into old age, grandkids and medical procedures, the Top Two one discusses over coffee with friends. And one day, I would have sickened, or one day I'd have fallen, and one day or night, I simply would have died. Each day alive until that time, takes away dreams, until dreams are all that remain. That's no riddle. I assume you know it already. In our end as creatures, all beauty and joy, is internal. It's what we conceive and husband. A something sometimes never fully known, and spoiled if it's birthed. There's only a dream, a reaching out for something which isn't there, and our breath is the engine that floats it, balloon. So, yes, I'm sorry. I would have been sorry, anyway. A man named Schoepenhauer, knew that—again, to dumb things down, he said that, if there exists no physical, human immortality, Here, Now, As We Are…fuck it. I'm no Pollyanna, never was. I don't have an answer for him.

Thus, dead alive, wrapped womb with alive dead, I breathe. She breathes. We. Together. Sometimes we kiss. Not often. But it happens.

Infantile human

The car isn't standard issue. It's a fun, tweaky blue, reserved for 'lectric kiddie cars of today's dying culture. Possibly Corvettes, ca. 1968. Past electraglide. Deep Blue. Like the computer a Russian chessmaster could beat, until Science Found a Way. Science, not exact and usually sneaky, cheats. As does US Intelligence.

"Mr. Teague?"

You don't turn. You don't hurry away, either. If the latter, the house will be surrounded, the neighborhood locked down within ten minutes. No power, no gas, no water. Though, this is small town Idaho. Town water operates on a system pre-WW2. Really, there's no depriving you of that one. But Intelligence finds a way.

"Good morning! Guy Wilson Teague?"

Your full name. No one gets called the whole mouthful, anymore. Maybe kids, whose moms equate old-fashioned with "cute". These cats aren't mothers, not that kind. Peripheral vision picks up dark coats, black shoe leather. Standard issue, these. Through channels, you know Smith and Atchisson supplies federal ordnance. Smith and Atchisson only creates things capable of clearing a college quad.

"Sir, we need you to stay, and to come on back."

Your driveway isn't long. By remaining parked barely out of sight, they spotted you and your morning paper a several step lead. But they've made the driveway as you hit the porch door, and the next statement will be a command.

You stop suddenly, hand to the knob, and they halt as fast, watchful but not yet defensive. You are 58 years old, a lumpy "dad"-type. You are clad in a bathrobe thick enough to pass as a raccoon coat. Your feet are bare, the swelled victims of blood pressure. Your hands are not in your pockets. There exists no reason for the agents, both male, to ante up.

"It's cold. I'm not awake," you tell them, a permitted grumble, given maturity. "Get to the bottom line."

The one at more than 90 degrees to and behind the other, answers over his shoulder.

"Mr. Teague, I'm Special Agent DeLillo, this is Agent Baum. We've flown all the way from Baltimore, I think you know why we're here."

Nooo, not at all. Of course you do. Theft, is why. Outright. Except, you're the thief. And not at all the original.

You're old, by your own reckoning. You own guns, all museum antiques, polished time in crystal cases. To this Union, you're made of paper. Still, you hesitate long enough, the junior agent, unwittingly a battlement for the other, pipes up.

"Sir, my partner and I have no interest in you personally. We hold no papers on you. There's no warrant. We've been dispatched here, to secure and retrieve the product."

That last word, an accurate description, still has the effect of a loogie in your face.

"'Product'". You echo it on the heels of a cringe.

DeLillo interposes, shoulder to shoulder now with Baum.

"Sir, we're not here to get personal. We want the item you have in your possession, which by rights belongs to the government of the United States. We ask you permit us entry to do retrieval ourselves. Barring that, you have leave to effect exit of the item using your own powers of persuasion, but be advised, we will have you on a strict, ten-minute time limit. Further, a six-man team is stationed in the woods to the rear, staggered, should there be trouble. I will appeal to you, this once: *Please cooperate fully.*"

You've wilted inside your "Ivy League game" robe. You know what's about to happen, and the regret deepest, is that regret combined with obedience, is all you are allowed. Your face displays this as you deflate, but these plus age, buy you seconds. Or ten minutes. You don't need either. But you do have a pound of flesh.

"I understand, agents. I'm aware; I'll get her. I do have a question, however, only one, very simple..."

Baum's brows arch.

"This isn't a game, sir."

Cold of tone, you tell him, "Oh, I *know* it's no game, son. And had you ever felt a *goddam* thing in your heart but loyalty and an honor beyond my comprehension, you'd know I know how real this is.

"I'm playing nothing. I have a question."

DeLillo shoulder-bumps his partner, a subtle silencing as he takes a forward half-step.

"Feel free to ask your question, Mr. Teague. I cannot guarantee either of us can furnish an answer."

Clever. Their patter, standard issue from their mouths, is practiced, which makes them perfect...'perfect', being relative and impossible. That's really what this is about.

"Why now?" you ask. "It's been sixteen years."

"It's an illegal possession, sir," answers DeLillo. "Sentient illegal, by the ability to make its own decisions...this fact, removes any real culpability on your part, assuming cooperation. As for the time period, the item was only traced here last week. Expiration, has been in mandate quite a long time, as I'm sure you're aware."

Yep. You sure are. You also know what that means. As do these young lions and their gang of guns off in the woods. You know as much as they all do, and a few things they don't. Things their betters guess at. Things long-dead men, theorized. Things you've been told, which you doubt yet believe. Guessing but knowing. Like Heaven, and untarnishing pennies with pre-80's Coke. All cards are now face up. Solitaire, three-way. You nod, start to request the ten minutes.

The inner door opens. Baum has a hand up at his lapel already, but DeLillo shoulder-bumps visibly and you wilt further as Linnette, looking young enough to surprise you, exits the porch and onto the top step.

"It's all right, husband," she says, sad, comforting. Resigned.

"It's never something gradual," she explains, as if you didn't know. "I'm not you, but I'm not a magazine subscription, either."

The Feds are silent, and frowning. They're permitting a fast farewell. Baum's hand is again at chest level. DeLillo makes no further correction.

"It isn't even right to say it," you tell your wife who isn't your wife, a woman never borne of woman.

"You get used to it," she says. White polish of complexion, pink tips of ears. Maybe 30 years old, maybe more. A snow girl who came out of Vermont, in 1943.

Adolf Hitler, killed millions. His vision, a maw of madness, terrified hundreds of millions. Linnette, more beautiful than any bomb, was supposed to have been The Bomb—rather, she was one attempt to avoid it. If her lean and leg and squirrel cheeks had proved the proverbial ticket, Earth would suffer thrice over from overpopulation. Steam heat and coal, would be global and unopposed. Train travel, for civilians, would predominate. And there would be no signals in the air.

"Wow," you tell this fantasy, a custom Stepford with bite. "Just, wow."

She leans to you, hands in the open, and you receive her likewise. Even at this, a hug all face and brush of lips, Agents Frick and Frack perceptibly react, observing as human cartoons.

"I liked you liking Linnette," she says in your ear, stage whisper. "I liked her, too. She was a good one."

"God bless the atomic bomb," you respond, tearful, as she plants a second kiss on the tip of your old nose.

The pair of you are eyes to eyes in gaze, satisfied at least in what each means to the other. Before either agent can crash the party, Linnette steps past you, hands upraised, into open space on the drive. The government then takes over and the commands begin as she is secured. Cuffed. Blindfolded, like a hostage. Sensor-equipped tape over her mouth. You know manacles will be applied in the vehicle, or once transferred to Federal holding. One agent tells you this is procedure; the other explains of contact, should any questions arise. Both thank you for your prompt cooperation, and DeLillo offers the olive branch of this being filed in your favor, assuming future need for a Get Out of Jail Free card. *Good ol' citizen. Thank 'ee. Here's a bone. And this is not a game.* Sure, Bert.

*Linnette", is not her name. She adopted it to please you, years ago. They're marching her to the street, to the deep blue midsize of nonstandard issue. Efficient as windup toys, they push her down, outsized luggage, into the back seat. Seconds later, you watch them drive away.

It's Sunday. Your community, with few exceptions, is churchly. Most of your neighbors are at worship. Only the man next door older than you, and the drunk in the corner house, were around to see. You assure the old man, whom sight of makes you think of death, that the arrest is a prank, part of the Policeman's Benevolent semiannual fundraiser. The drunk, you convince had seen a prowler arrested. Not Mrs. Teague.

This all happened at ten in the morning. As shadows deepen that afternoon, you're alone in the den. Looking at photographs, watching home videos. Of your life, perhaps the past 40 years of it. Of you and Linnette, or whatever name you like- –she told you the Montpelier team realizing her, used "Sarah Kay", to aid identity. The 'K'-part, was the first letter of a product code on the small hatch at the base of her spine. In an upsetting escapade you've tried to forget, she had you burn away the code and registry stamp, many years ago. Plastic surgery was unnecessary.

Linnette is not your sole and only love. Photos of her, magnetic tape of you two moving here, of Christmases, melts with speed as you review your life. Here is Bree, a sickly-looking anorexic you lived with in California. Not one photo, where she doesn't look like she's riding on about two hours' sleep. Well, maybe the Halloween pic with the werewolf makeup.

Further distant, and here's Wanda, biker babe and prostitute. Usually in a casual state of undress. The legs look like trench warfare between cellulite and muscle, but in truth, she could kick a person to death. You watched her do that, once. Fastest relocation you ever pulled.

The "memory lane"-bit, a pity party your just due, goes on until well after 9 P.M. No interruptions, but for the drunk on the corner (*"Are you sure...?"*). You have plenty of time to think about love and warmth and life and emptiness. About "real". In the end, it's what a person wishes. The pundits and talking heads deride any true, hardcore self-esteem. But this far into the 21st Century, it's the stuff of what human is. What they want. You are what you choose, so to speak. Hoary Voices of Reason, be silent.

It's late, or feels it. You put visuals of your life away, as youth and the background of youth trend toward high school. Your love there, was your First: "Lorna". The realest of your life. You can't look at that time, not often, as your emotions never truly healed. High school loves, tend to collapse. Only a handful are ever realized. You blundered into your 20's with a lot of anger. The one time you ever used a gun in violence, was when you rented the Brooke Shields movie, *Endless Love*. The television tube exploded with such force, the drapes caught fire. Elvis would have been proud.

You wanted done with "real", after that. Harmed once, you decided love was bullshit. You can't even conscien Good and Bad in the same package. Again, perfection is unattainable. People, human beings, are Lucy from Schulz' *Peanuts*: you hold the football, and they come running up and kick you. A creature like Linnette...Sarah Kay, whoever...is a miracle. Many, most, would damn such a thing, some out of fear, but most via the precious fool's gold of their own "nobility". The agents and their "honor". High concepts with a fine ring, until they collapse when imperfect Human shifts into 2nd. Any Other Human, especially. Everyone's always fine, in a sleep tube of their own.

The only thing positive about high-minded thinking, is that Utopian dreams, ideals set by oath, the best, shiniest efforts and attitudes, are seldom criminal. "Positive", yeah, there's another one. Positive as glaze, as mantra, *The Little Engine That Could* in a story you slept by, vague and general and nebulous "encouragement" which pats you on the back and doesn't want your drama. Plato, and his "good emotions". Cold War school marm lines in the sand. And a poor defense, should Court actually materialize. Human beings are trash to you, and apes and low sorts of things. It took something better for you, a thing you are not allowed. You, it requires no emphasis, do not care what you're allowed. The 'what' doesn't care, either.

You've replaced the visuals, out of focus, poor quality of your life, into storage. The storage area itself, is military in format and in its accessibility. Easy to find things, easy to move them. To bug out. The antique guns sealed in their crystal cases, you'll have to abandon. That's fine. You'd rather have endless love.

Bedtime is always prompt at midnight. Before you lie down, you leave the back porch screen open and ajar. In bed then, boy waiting for Santa, never doubting...but in grip of the Sandman, sleep prevails.

The noise, uneven, animal, distressed, a struggling, wakes you into murk. Your eyes don't work as once they did. The room is soup, except for the clock. **4:17**. Only the time of year has it pitch, past the windows. Though you own the back quarter acre, plenty of eyes are up, washed of sleep, ramping for work. You don't bother to dress.

You go to the kitchen, which accesses the back porch, and with fingertips, tap a code. After seconds, this is repeated by you, with an extra "shave and a haircut". The repeat of this in return, is laborious. The thing is in pain. You know this task was Herculean even for it. As you open to its raw reality, you think of suffering and love, suffering *for* love. You think of *Lassie, Come Home*.

It has to slither in. You assist, by pulling. Its red is mud brown, its blue is gunmetal grey. There is little blood remaining, but its wounds are self-flushed and cauterized. You will be told later, it had to produce a new head. There will be a lot of hard tales, as there have been before. Again, you feel ironic regret. For the agents, who only thought they knew. Baum, especially. He froze at point blank, she'll tell you, when her new head popped suddenly out, and just as suddenly his was popped off. Foolish, you've always thought that. Dying for a speech out of a Captain America comic. No words on this Earth, keep one warm.

You tend the thing in the narrow kitchen, on the floor. Bring what chemicals nourish it best. Humming, which it likes. Singing songs of childhood years, but from your mother's day. By the time the kitchen, a windowless room, is bright from the light in all others, it can stand. The throwdown, you'll be told, took place an hour past Miles City, Montana. It...*she*, ran hundreds of miles to rejoin you so quickly, every so often teleporting forward. Something better. The product of WW2 genetic tinkering married with hard technics as new and a mysticism now vanished off the planet. A differently-abled actualized in full.

This miracle retires to the basement, a place you never visit. Without ceremony, you crash, wondering only how much time the pair of you have to disappear. The creature in a calculated intelligence, would have left behind confusing clues, good for misdirection and delay, but US Intelligence, if it makes use of any superstition in its arsenal, takes that trick. The Information Age can be muck rather than grease for these people, but overconfidence will no longer show its face.

You don't wonder or even question to whom you'll awaken. Linnette told you, long ago. She had been "Ann", some aggressive MILF far too old for you, when she had brought love to someone who overvalued such an imperfect thing. Ann, though, was often as young as 20's or as old as you are now, the aging up and down like a piano solo, used to nurture, and to teach. You didn't improve, nor did you grow or mature, but during this long experiment of her own, the creature decided she liked caregiving. Those with whom she had been since escaping post-Project confinement in the 1950's, had only ever controlled and used. The creature never confided in any of them. She told no one the truth, before you.

Right before she adopted "Wanda", sensing the Feds were closing in, she opened her heart to you. Told you everything, and pure. She as thing, has organic mechanism, a perpetual motion wrought from Nature and bent to the laws of the lab. This amalgam of an engine—one reason the project was killed—is fused with a like central nervous system. Not a favorite of Old Detroit, or any who pray to the god of Planned Obsolescence. Her skin cells are malleable for appearance, but the overall mold is hard. You were told, decades ago, *"When I begin to let you choose, don't choose often."*

You didn't. "Bree", was her idea as well. Both Bree and Wanda, were street people she had met. The creature has known homelessness, and hunger for lab chemicals is still hunger. You took care of her in turnabout, as you were able. Ann, then Wanda, then Bree, then Linnette, took care of you. Linnette was a jockette you once knew. The only one who'd ever stirred you, beside Lorna. This was when you thought everything between lovers was real and sincere, full face. The two elements, reality and sincerity, often do not go together. You got lucky. Yes, you did. Even if the 'who' is an it, and a very illegal possession.

Gambling, or perhaps inheritance, are the only luck which give money. Until 16 years ago and Linnette—your choice of mold, a gift—the pair of you lived poor, sometimes desperate. Wanda, as stated, prostituted. The guy she kicked to death, was an undercover agent posing as a john. She was Bree within days, and you two were already states away. Crime pays. It bought you your fine home and antiques, way up in northern Idaho. The creature always did any dirty work. She could fight and survive, and live on; you, very mortal, probably could not. That was another reason they killed the project. Once the war was over, how did you get rid of these things? An army had been planned. They only made Sarah Kay.

You sleep what for you, is a very long time. You awake in thick of the after-noon, cuddled against your wife, your woman who is neither. It takes only your old eyes focusing, which even in natural light takes a moment, to know you hold Lorna, and you know you will hold her for life. It doesn't matter if the government breaks down the door, doesn't matter weapons and violence, a going away into darkness or light. By choice, reality as dream, the she-crea-ture now gives you dream as reality. She gives this freely. A balm, to pacify fear.

You're an accomplice at last. One way or another. This reverts back to Ann in her role those early days. Mom, taking care. Being good to a man because he is good to her. Simple, transactional. This is understood. The way people used to be. Her super intellect long ago concluded only simplicity, free give and take without betrayal, allows for harmony and thus, embrace. Happiness as immutable. You've never claimed super intellect, but your conclusion was ever the same. *"Do unto others, as you are done unto."* The Passive-Aggressive Golden Rule. Stimulus A can *only* produce Response B. As Bree, she once told you that she loved you were like a warm computer. You said you didn't know computers were passive-aggressive.

It takes 2 days to pack and load a van with altered plates. You sell your antique guns to the concern out back of the hunting lodge. Downtime is spent in bed, but most is just affection. The so-called product, your illegal "item", speaks of Life ahead, of how she will take care of everything, every detail. Take care of you, until you die. She can't make you like her, of course. Neither can you end what will be her near-immortal suffering. But it's like that, even when it works out. You, anyone, aren't perfect. Life, humankind, the world. Your standards are rather higher than norm. You got lucky, pal. No matter who you see next to you, never forget that.

By Thursday, predawn, you're on the road. The Feds don't know Lorna from a load of hay. You keep your mirrored shades on, sun visor pulled to the side. Jacket, hooded. There are always risks. Lorna has her sights set on Kansas; there's a tourist trap which might serve. Today her eyes sag, and her cheeks are drawn. She could easily be your age. Tonight? 17, 20. 28. Something else.

While on the interstate, you lament, re: law and crime. Lorna tells you both are grounded firmly in not disturbing others. That the cycle in case of your pair bond is endless, is natural.

"Didn't we start it, though?" you counterpoint, all human.

"Did we?" she's quick in riposte. "They would blow it off as an infantile reasoning, but neither one of us asked to be here. We're beings outside the circle, forced to survive. It's this, or suicide."

You don't answer. A mile goes by. Lorna glances, then stares your way.

"At least you're gonna get to leave."

You lock eyes. She is not watching the road, but you know she can look away a whole minute, and stay within the lane. Her now-blue eyes are serious. It's been 40 years. You know she means no harm.

"You want to drive this off the next embankment?", you suggest, perhaps half joking.

A brief hesitation, then blue eyes back on the road. Her driving is without flaw. The van hasn't strayed. It needs no correcting. A machine, guided by a kind of one. A better thing. An idea Science once had. Until it decided radioactive bombs were less threatening. Lorna smiles, taking in your dare. Happy, sad. Rueful.

"*No*," she says. "I don't want to be alone."

The Breaking of Eternity by Time

There are two police precincts in Fabron Isles, California, Coastal and Inland. Any records archived in the old way, are stored at Inland Precinct, lower level. A data storage area erroneously named "Computer Room B", contains all records held only in physical form. These, are of persons unknown, from times and happenings unspoken. There are items fanciful and hard evidence of the legendary as detective work, archived, numbered, filed. Among the many arcane, cryptic and sometimes impossible records, there stands a deep filing cabinet of two drawers. The bottom drawer is labeled, "Dissenters". Most of the casefiles within, are stamped "CLOSED", in green, also with two very different seals, both ostensibly of the State of California.

One file unstamped, a case considered active therefore pursuable, contains a formal wedding portrait, dating to 1922. A young man in tails, gloved, chin high and at the tilt, stands left of and discernibly apart from his bride, who is seated upon a short, squat divan, facing him in profile. The woman, hair appearing bright white due to the style of photography, is in period trousseau, but for her veil, a modified version of that worn by brides in biblical times. In the portrait, her eyes show closed and she seems to mourn, head bowed in respect to her detached, proud husband. The wedding rings of both are visible. The jewels inset, are not diamonds, but show as black.

On the floor before the couple, just identifiable enough as the foreground is cut off, is stretched an animal skin rug with full head, centered before them. The animal is a wolf. It is indeed dead. It is not a rug.

The team had labored in the abandoned elegance past the city's north end, for over a month. Sizzlin' Demo and Contractors. The firm was local, so to them came the big jobs, like any time developers managed to score a piece to the north and west. Old Fabron Isles. The remains of a fire from the time of JFK, or sweet, Edwardian houses unused, greatgrandaddy to urban decay. Tearing down overdone, leviathan beauty dried to rot through sea salt and emptiness. Without a pang of remorse. Without thought. Those of collars blue, knew nothing was forever. If you wanted to play pretend, take care of your stuff.

Nels Blaine, roving crew chief ("troubleshooter" or "snitch", depending on whether you liked the guy), was finishing a few last shots with his phone, of what, 4 weeks before, had been a murky row of dead history called Song Place. Blaine had taken pix every few days as the street, perpendicular to where they were working, had gone away physically as well, bones removed from bloodless things. He didn't know what he'd do with the stuff, he wasn't dumb enough to say "write a book", and social media bored him. Blaine nonetheless had made time as lightless lumps and sticks of homes had become a field of straw pressed to mud. Many yards on, this tufted to green and the gristle-glint of hot sand until it hit the access road. The space, not attractive, was now at least, wide open. What was coming, good plan or bad, would have its day. Song Place was in landfills, counties away, and in the air.

They were about a third down Feather Street, same crypts of America Past, too big and too close to the ocean. No mighty earthquake had taken down even one, but this was northern California, anyway, above even the Napa Valley. A part of the state the other parts seldom counted. Middle class and traditional. Some lingering, Wild West roots. Slightly manic-depressive. The citizens of Fabron Isles traveled and returned, but few outsiders made a point to visit. There existed no Welcome Center. Not even on the Internet.

Blaine pocketed his phone after checking Notifications, turning as his name was called.

It was Dillman, electrics specialist, waving and pointing. He indicated the tallest structure on Feather Street, #2001, three-quarters down from where Blaine stood. The foreman, Mr. Thorson, once Song Place was carted off, had directed the crew, double-sized, to take out the middle section of what remained, homes backyard ass to each other. The ones working the other side, facing Wind Street, had been much slower. The foreman had told Blaine twenty minutes ago, to keep watch there and kick the necessary dogging butts. Dealing with Dillman's issue would slow that process, but so did Blaine's wistful photo-clicking, so...

"I'm just in 2001," said Dillman as they met up. "It's next, but everyone's on material cleanup in 2005. Those attic planks are barely deteriorated, you know, I was surprised, they could be used for someth..."

"Take that up with Thorson," said Blaine. "What you got?"

"'Way down below'-issue. Sub-subbasement, the ones dug for drainage failsafe."

"Yeah? We got mass Pacific sewage?"

"No," said Dillman as Blaine quickened his pace.

"Then, what?"

"The sub-subs were only ever drainage, most often you had a 19th Century force-flush option. Possibly, you'd have pipes extending that low, but never anything else. Not electrics, not gas. Nothing."

Blaine stopped. They stood in blackgreen rags of fat weeds, once a lawn.

"So? What? I got shit to do, Dillman. You found Black Bart's cave? What?"

The specialist gestured with an arm wrapped in doublethick connector cable.

"You got a power source down there."

The men, neither seeking further help, were fast down the ladder which descended from the lower floor, sawn through to specifically accommodate, then below basement level, through a crawlspace wedge of subbasement—all of these buttressed with sandwiched layers of wood, rock, uneven filler, and industrial antiquities far worse than asbestos. Dillman already had campfire lamps at the bottom, also a halogen suspended from a mini scaffolding. The air was what it was—you got used to a cornucopia of stink at this job—but there had been initial cleanup, a sweep through to prevent stupid accidents, like stepping on tetanus. Blaine stopped as soon as he turned. He sidled. Stared at the central wall.

"There's been no city hookup even for light in these blocks, since maybe Nixon," Dillman was saying. "The power source is behind that granite, but it has nothing to do with the house itself. I hadn't come across a wall that big, it takes up almost all room down here but the walkways, goes in a square, all around! No 2nd subbasement I've ever seen, and it's drier down here than any I've checked."

"Supporting walls?" asked Blaine, circumnavigating, flashlight in hand. He knew they weren't.

"Well, no, sir, there's nothing to support! What, support the buffer to the 1st subbasement? That's a crawl area, nothing more. Barely that.

"I've only lived here six years, and there's too much weirdo in Fabron Isles," Dillman went on. "I've got stuck with jobs at Remnant Hill. There aren't enough benefits for the shit. I don't like scary movies, either, even mysteries!"

Blaine heard that. No one liked working jobs on Remnant Hill, though the neighborhoods were so cloistered, you seldom had one. The abandoned stretch just north, was neither cloistered nor unfriendly, nothing shadowy or cold about these high houses. No one contemptuous of questions, but no one to answer them, either. The big, too-Midwestern barns of houses, had indeed no occupants of record since Richard Nixon ruled the Earth. And no one, even the men bordering on retirement, asses stuck in driver's seats of machinery, remembered a time when Song Place and Wind Street and Feather Street had been a populous, active part of Fabron Isles. Like everything north and hugging the ocean, the neighborhoods were dead, but these elder giants housed no crime. They housed nothing much higher on the scale, than lizards. Occasionally, a bird, and superstitious men would take a personal day on the spot, reminding they couldn't be fired, as they were union.

Blaine felt of the stone while on the far side. Impressive stuff. Red granite, hand chiseled. The walls, 12' x 12'—you learned early, to eye it. Once he'd rejoined Dillman and playing a hunch, they inspected, hand and penlight, to find the blocks, great of size, matched seamless, to one another. There had been a red stone quarry much further inland, shut down in the 1950's. To match handcut blocks where no one would look to see...the hydraulics involved, for this deep...

Dillman had, before buttonholing Blaine, asked for go ahead on drilling test holes, in case of gas. Blaine next had Dillman retrieve the crew's top shelf industrial diamond tip, the largest on hand. Once returned, Dillman appointed himself to only a supporting role, and until lunch, again after, they worked alone in the centralized depths. Gloved. Goggled. Insulated. Often leaned into the wall.

Procedure called for two holes drilled before a chemical test. Nels Blaine, superstitious by nature, always drilled three. He forced himself to not look into the room, for a room it was, and brightly lit. Dillman, keeping strict watch, announced the first color seen as red, then more signs of it, then mixed with halogen white. The two colors varied with drillwork, but once finished and the drill withdrawn for good, only the bright white was reported, which fast dimmed to low wattage incandescence.

Both requisite chemical test from the minilab in the site trailer and old fashioned sniff tests, showed no danger. The air in fact had begun toward fresh and mild, rancid stink pushed back.

Dillman said he was "pretty hot to see" what was inside, but a call came for him, informing his kid was very sick and had been sent home from school. Blaine, feeling strange for no reason about sharing the moment, of course had him clock off, but it was nearly quitting time, before he felt ready to peer into the confines of the red granite walls. After he did, as a gawker at a freak show or small child spying on the amores of parents, Blaine had to keep pulling his face from the peep hole every few minutes. Blinking. Shaking head. Rubbing eyes. Fascinated, and very afraid.

Inside the small citadel of red granite, lit well enough still from Blaine's angle, was what appeared to be a prop, cliché and stock, from a very dated scifi movie set. Artistically pleasing perhaps, ornate, it reeked of the worst, 70's camp. Colors, angles, contours, accoutrements and superfluous gadgetry. A jackhole imitation of the fantastical. Right down to the captive guest star. The reason Blaine kept looking away, then back.

Female, blonde. Medium height. Retro hairstyle. Ivory skin. Suited neckline to toe in another cliché, the infamous grey leotard. Suspended akimbo, hooked into the machine as a human "X". Color in her cheeks. Breathing without strain. If you played it as fantasy and "wrote the story", the woman had been imprisoned. There was otherwise no entrance to this tomb. Great blocks from a quarry gone before Blaine had been born, aligned fitted, precise. The woman, soft milk of curves, had a look about her Nels Blaine knew well. The striking "old fashioned face". Sweet which was stalwart, gentility cut with tradition. The beauty, proud. The sort you found in old photos and portraits, from the time these homes had thrived.

He kept staring and rubbing eyes, staring and shaking head, even smacking his face and stamping feet before staring into the drill hole again. Quitting time came and went. It was after 7, when he left the site. His hips hurt, from standing so long in one position.

Nels Blaine put the sight away when he went back to his home life, but it kept re-emerging. Unreal. Surreal. Too big, too big. Newsworthy, which he didn't like. He knew he didn't have to get further involved, but within a day or two, he'd have to report it, as the men would continue according to plan as dictated by the foreman. Blaine figured he had to talk with Thorson, he had the authority to approach, but his superior was one for delegating and hanging back. Then again, unlike many Blaine had worked for, Thorson was at least even tempered. Nonetheless, when he stood at Thorson's trailer desk next morning, no one else present, five minutes into the workday, Blaine could only blunder into the topic.

Following a report on random concerns, he asked the foreman, a man permanently burnt by the sun, "Who owned these lots, before the City?"

Thorson blinked.

"Majus or Wineman, they're the big dogs. I would guess. If a small fry, there's generally dumb special instructions, and Rosecrux homes, no one touches. So, Wineman. Majus. Why?"

"Before then, though?"

"Blaine, why do you give a fuck? What is this?"

And Blaine told him.

Ten minutes after Blaine related the tale, the foreman was lifting his own, spying eye from the drill hole. Scared, very much the shitless variety.

"I'll check City Records in person," he said, not looking at Blaine. "I wouldn't dare go to company directly. *Don't you.*"

"No problem," said Blaine. "No death wish, here."

Thorson swallowed, a sick noise.

"Throw this crew onto Wind Street," he ordered. "No one down here, de-prioritize anything on this block but clean up. I'm downtown to City, but keep me on the clock. Any delay, punch me out about two minutes late."

"No problem," Blaine said once more.

"Oh, there's a problem," Thorson told him, brushing past. "For me and you, especially."

The drive to City Hall from the work site was not a short one, and given bad luck, Thorson might have to stand in line. Blaine, however, didn't begin to see the trip necessitating punching his boss out. Yet the foreman returned not a quarter hour after everyone knocked off, and not two minutes after Blaine was alone in the trailer, waiting. Blaine made banter ("you just missed all the work"), but Thorson had in fact not walked into City Hall until it was almost ready to close.

"End of the day, they have skeleton crews in any department," he said. "Usually just one person to a counter. A lot of times, they have to see you first, then walk up. I wanted this to be as 'nothing' as could be arranged."

They sat, and Blaine read the home's factual history. A "Guy W. Teague" had purchased 2001 Feather Street outright, in 1918. The place had gone for taxes, during the heart of the Depression. The clerk on initiative had been good enough to find a descendent living in town, and all this was very well. But, an elderly woman in the department, had heard their conversation, and she—also on initiative—politely butted in right before Thorson could step away. Smiling and helpful as any grandmother remembered. The woman reached around her younger coworker, handing Thorson a manila folder containing a photostat, a blown up portion of an antique portrait.

"That's him!", she said, bright and nice. "That's taken from a Ventox, that portrait, they don't come out in copies too good unless you, you know, enlarge them a lot."

"What?" Thorson had said, and the coworker, turning only head, eyes downcast more than looking at the old woman, said, "I'm sorry, what was that you said?"

Barely "one-Mississippi", and helpful Gramma answered the latter with, "I said nothing. I left at 4. I was just handin' 'im 'ee's picture."

"How was she there, if she'd left at 4:00?" Blaine wanted to know as Thorson rose to hand him the folder.

"Covering her tracks," said Thorson. "I don't want to go into it. In Fabron Isles, there's wonky shit. The older it's about, the wonkier it is."

Blaine took the file, opening to the blowup. He agreed more than ever, about the weird and the wonky. Certainly, about the "shit". He held the copy nearer the desk lamp. Standard dapper don of the 20's, looked like, although the style of photography could be older than that. He couldn't tell if the portrait was badly shot or the granny's copy poorly run off. Blaine began to ask what was a "Ventox", but Thorson's next words shanked the whole conversation.

Thorson said, "I saw this joker pictured, at Ruhlin's. My anniversary was last week, wife dines high end on any occasion she can. Spot on, looked just like in this. Like he should have existed as black and white. Some starved blonde at his table, Twiggy meets The Wolfman. Anyway, I remember. Mainly because of his clothes. 'I'm Rudolph Valentino', like that."

They sat, staring at one another.

Blaine, reasoning, said, "So, he owned...this Teague-dude owned this home, starting in 1918. This photo, says 1922. The home was taken for back taxes, in the early 30's. It's 80 years later, and you see him chowing at Ruhlin's."

Without directly answering, Thorson said, "I don't want sucked into this, but we need that woman out of there before next week. We can keep Chubs Dillman from peeking, lie out the ass, he'll never be on *Jeopardy*, but..."

"Blaine, I don't want any part of the fallout. Whoever holds the ace. Company, media or both."

"Agree!" said Blaine. "...but, I don't know how we find the Eternal Man, here. Or his greatgrandson, whoever your fashion buster was."

The foreman looked ill, and like he wanted to cry, and as though blue uniforms were reading him Miranda Rights, and for that, annoyed his life had been complicated.

He dug two fingers, pincer, into his shirt pocket, withdrawing a folded piece of decorative memo paper. He breathed out, unhappy, frustrated, as he leaned across the desk without rising. He didn't look at Blaine as the crew chief received it.

"My brother's a lot younger than me. He knows better, how technics work. The Web. My brother's also an amoral asshole. So he knows how to use the Web like you shouldn't. He said he crosschecked. The man's at that address, or we got mass shit, tomorrow."

Another old neighborhood, not a good one. Fender Street. There were other stories about that section. Mainly though, it was just shanty. Or had grown so. The name above the address, "Guy W. Teague." Blaine squinted at Thorson, cockeyed.

"*Who?*"

"There's such things as namesakes," said Thorson. "Legacies. Get going. And thanks for the shitty Monday."

Via text that evening, the foreman granted Blaine a personal day. At ten the next morning, the crew chief was parking in another old part of Fabron Isles. The city consisted of almost nothing but detached sections which were conceived, built, rose, thrived, decayed and fell into spooky ruin. A series of modern ancient civilizations in the form of neighborhoods, none of them going back much further than California Statehood. The only decent places to live, here, represented on a map, showed as fresh mortar connecting dead bricks. Unlike the other "bricks", this place had just died within the past twenty years. It was a place drained and pitted. Still harmless, but waiting for the crime.

The home in question, was built on a slant of noticeable incline. High ground. By date, not much newer than the dark of Feather Street. Broad steps from curb to sidewalk, sidewalk to front walkway, walkway to porch. The porch steps looked like someone had at them with a tenderizing mallet.

After a minute, the door was answered, and by the man in the antique "Ventox". Almost a copy of his photograph, or whosoever it was. An art deco face with a speakeasy haircut. Blaine introduced himself, then,

"Are you Guy Teague? Guy W. Teague?"

The face remained what it was, but the eyes, which had been hazel, held mud in them.

"Do I know you?" came careful words.

Quickshot, Blaine explained his job and where the company had been working. Something about this seemed to peel back Teague's face, a slowmo of reaction to a gun going off, or very lagging shock. Blaine got as far as "2001", and Teague reached in greeting, to near-pull him into the foyer. Blaine turned to see Teague looking out the large glass of the front door, studying.

"I came alone," he told his host, and Guy Teague became at once the pinnacle of normalcy. He walked Blaine to the livingroom, bade him sit, then excused himself, thumb jerked at a closed, lacquered swivel door.

"I'm on the phone," said Teague. "You'll forgive me."

"Hey, no problem," said Blaine, taking a seat in an overstuffed green chair. Knowing somehow he was supposed to be parked. Still, secured. That Teague waited until he had sat back to smile and nod (approval?), let alone leave the room, told Blaine something about the man.

He waited. Teague was no more than another room distant. His tone with the other party on the phone was quiet but unpleasant. Nels Blaine took in his surroundings. Like many places in Fabron Isles, this home was out of date. Like most, owners could have been taken better care. There was the burden of age, of drowning quiet seeping from the walls. Every one of the few sticks of furniture or few wall adornments, were out of place. Not shabby, only a little, but things of far gone vintage kept useful, handy. Living, in a dead room. Blaine remembered his grandmother's apartment. Elder things she wouldn't let him touch. Coupled with Teague's voice near-distant, now going up an octave in menace, nervous energy made the workman stand. He moved about the troubling room.

The couch across from his chair was immense and horsehair, a true relic. Blaine inspected a nearby drinks trolley. A decanter of fine crystal, weighted stopper sculpted as the head of the holy madonna, ringed with starburst. Finest detail. All features were sculpted. Fangs included.

An art deco table sat under a clouded mirror. The table had seen better days; overpolishing had made it look like chocolate bars. A single white business card with red and gold logo, looked up at him, bold, *faux*-roadside Indian kitsch.

"Lincoln & Fin's", in contoured font upon a war drum. This clicked immediately. A clutch of love 'em and leave 'em cottages, several miles inland. Blaine had heard the usual sordid stories. Hey, whatever turned you on.

He heard Teague in the next room, syllables bitten, not at all friendly. There was a dialect unknown, and in a rush, the conversation ended. Unprepared, Blaine put distance between himself and the doorway to the kitchen. He'd just managed to turn around by the green chair, before the swivel door swiveled.

"Okay!" his host said on entrance. "Now I've reminded a client what day this is, I can hear you. Since we've never met, I get a feeling this is about me, not what I do. That's never good. But speak your piece."

Eye contact. Teague this time pointed Blaine to sit, looked about, and in a smooth motion scooped up the screw-cabins business card as though dealt it, slipping it cupped, into a front pocket. Only then did Blaine notice the freshly pressed, thigh-baggy cut of Teague's pants. Very dapper, pomade and dancing the Charleston. It always took all kinds, but, please.

Teague made no offer of refreshment (Blaine could smell his, three feet away; who took crème de menthe, neat?), and sat angling, a foot tucked, on the horsehair davenport. His goblet, cut glass polished to burnish, was palmed. The man gestured with it. His eyes were troubled, and at first grew darker, but softened as Blaine continued, lids at length lowering to hide any reaction. He ended looking at his lap, in seeming debate with himself. When Blaine hit the punchline of "Do you know who this woman is?", Teague nodded to himself to punctuate, and his face broadened with a certain pride.

"That's my wife. Her name, is Lorna."

Pride more. An odd happiness, too, but Blaine caught it as whimsy. The man was off a step, maybe. Not yet mad.

Blaine asked, "How long have you been married?"

Teague opened his mouth, then faltered.

"It would be tough to explain, and tougher to understand, but I'll try it this way: have you ever heard of a local cathedral, 'The Shrine of St. Linus'?"

"Uhm."

Blaine wished Thorson the townie, had come along. The reference, arcane, Blaine had heard. Once. Halloween, when son Brett came home babbling bullshit older kids were spinning.

"I might have heard the name," he said. "I don't know where it is. Not around here."

"Do you know where Mother Seton Church, is?"

Blaine nodded.

"Sure, south end, as houses thin out. Just before the rock beach."

"Very good!" said Teague, with new life. "And, before it was built in '83, the lot held burned ruins dating to 1962. St. Boniface of Glory."

"I'd heard about that."

And he had, but a church gone since the Cuban Missile Crisis was too far in the past for where Teague seemed to be leading.

"You're maybe 30," Blaine said.

Guy pushed himself up, perching atop the back of the horsehair like an antsy frat boy.

"Uhh*yeahh*...I'm not as old as I used to be, you pardon me. St. Boniface isn't where I'm going. You see, it was built back in 1936, but anyone and every-one will say, and most won't have to think when they say it, St. Boniface was 101 years old, when it went up. Fact is, it stood only the 26 years. Until 1931, the church on the ground, was the Shrine of St. Linus. Lorna and I were sealed there—it was called sealed, in that time—sealed through vows eternal and through all dimension, on the 28th day of October, 1922."

Silence for several minutes. Blaine stared at the man, looked around the room. Made a face or two. Teague sipped his drink. Smiled into it a few times.

It was Guy who finally spoke.

"I'll ask something I shouldn't, and you give me only yea or nay. Depending where you're from, this might register deep or shallow...did you hear, growing up, from family, in school, among close friends, the term "original timeline"? "Original history"? "The First History"? "Real Earth", anything like that?"

The key turned, a skeleton key of brass. Blaine's first day of kindergarten, back in Illinois, the wrinkled basset hound of a teacher. "Mrs. Faulhaver". Her voice the bleat of an old sheep, telling them all, warning of "the one 'NO'"...how there had been a world of creations, of histories, where myth was not myth, a vastly different Earth and America (called "Columbia"), which had been, by diplomatic agreement, erased, some decades past. Rewritten, censored and added to, edited and padded. All peoples and nations and tongues paved over in a planetary change, a remodeling. Destroying and remaking, at once. Humanity, in full accord that humankind and its accumulated detail through the aeons, be utterly, utterly changed. Made new. Persons living at that time, yes, it had been 1931 and 2, were held unbelievably to an honor system, subject to immediate removal upon the smallest infraction. Anyone who spoke of The World That Then Was, past asking in the manner Guy Teague asked Blaine now, went away. That's how it had been said by Mrs. Faulhaver, the wrinkled basset hound and kindergarten teacher. The bleat of an eyewitness to a cleansing storm. *Please be good, children...please don't don't go away.*

"Yes," he answered, sounding like the small boy he'd been.

Guy Teague looked older now, and wise.

"Good," he said. "That's fine. Well, Lorna and I were happy—happiness as contentment, a virtuous state in that time—until not long after our 8th Anniversary. We were rearing a family, involved in our church, contributing, making sacrifice and whole burnt offering...see, me even saying that, should clue you. It's the seeds of me looking as young as you, yet it's four score and twelve, since we were adjudged. Dissenters were eliminated, openly and regularly, until after what you know as WW2. In the 30's, in a place even this scattered away from larger influence, a person went away every few weeks."

He stopped, and studied Blaine. Sipping from the goblet, watching the man restrain himself from asking, a seeking which would even today, incriminate. And still punished in the ancient way.

Teague said, "Time travelers from the 2400's saved us. We were in our pit cell. The great drum had begun the prelude. I know this is garble to you, son. Gibberish. Thank God as you know Him, you don't understand.

"We were terrified of the new beings, their arrival, but more so of dying. We went with our savior-friends, to 2426. It was a new place yet again, but only in bureaucracy. We were obliged to marry again, vowing blood allegiance to State Over Life. Let alone each other. The entire process, took us into 2427. We felt we'd sold our souls.

"There was no place for us in the far future, not in the remade past. Lorna asked our saviors, still very much friends, to take us back, even further back, into a world and reality we understood. Terrified of the state, they refused, but I believe they loved us, as the chief control mechanism, always locked away, was left in plain sight, our next visit."

The gravity of the tale accounted for another silence. Blaine fidgeted and Teague drank. At some point,

"We by now knew how the time unit worked, but operating with any precision was a perfect art. We tried for the late 19th Century, before we'd have been born, to be safe. We wound up in the wettest Spring you could imagine, in 1918. I assume you know a little History.

"My immunity was always second to none. Lorna died of influenza, after 3 weeks."

Blaine, rather than make eye contact or another face, stared at his toes.

Teague said, "What you're seeing in the "core" or "depth core" as it was called, the holiest part of a home or often, a prison...what you're seeing, is Lorna remade. The space-y stuff, was culled from our time unit. There were instructions for building time preservation, a stasis area. I had about five days to construct it, once I knew she was dying for real."

"Th-the flu-plague thing really happened, though?" Blaine asked, wondering. Feeling bad such a question mattered to him.

Guy Teague smiled with rue. Almost, with jade.

"Wellll...c'mon! They didn't junk the whole works. Many things maintained an integral place. For what it's worth, from Thomas Jefferson up to Lincoln are the same order of the Presidents, and Edison really invented the light bulb. Oh, there's lots of real stuff kept around, lots of History happened, the Louisiana Purchase, everything. And the 1918 flu epidemic, was real. And she died."

Blaine started. "B...! But, you saved her!"

"Only as long as she's hooked into time preservation," said Teague. The man was grim. Perhaps not as grim as he should have seemed.

"It's hard for you to know, like I say," he told Blaine. "Lorna died, about six or seven hours before I could get her connected up...but the tiniest adjustment on the controls, and she was alive, again! Six or seven hours behind you and me, but as I keep saying, it's confusing."

Interjecting, Blaine asked, fast, direct, "What about yourself?"

He looked Teague, the couch rider, up and down.

"You're maybe 30," said, repeating his assessment in a different tone. "How were *you* preserved?"

Teague rolled eyes, with a smile. The "Devil may care"-sort. Any illusions he'd created, were incinerated, magnesium-style. Blaine, in seeing what was in the man's face, knew the problem at 2001 as much worse.

Said Teague, "I lived here, until 1925. Our friends came, in a new unit. The State, that cruel one from the Future, had grown even more oppressive, more...'Orwellian', how's that one? George Orwell, by the way, wrote those frightening visions down, in the late 1920's. They were later accepted, with necessary altering of dates, into the Remade Earth. There's another giftie for you. Mum's the word.

"Speed, is the doormat of spacetime. Dimension plays a part, but basically, go fast enough and you can hit Reverse. My friend and I have traveled for over 100 years. We live somewhen for awhile, enjoy as we may, then take to spacetime, again. Enjoy an "age diet", along the way. If our unit is kept hatbox fresh, ship and shape, there's very nearly a "forever" in the equation."

Blaine should have at least been impressed to his socks by the revelation. The possibilities should have evoked jealousy or friendly envy. A respectful request for relocation in Time. "Teach me how", anything. The workman could only fixate on the image of the stranded traveler in the...core...chained, effectively, to life support. Alone. And, who cared? The man he sat with, sat blameless, one to whom culpability was a stranger. *I didn't kill her, did I? I saved her life.* But a word, a tense spoken already, made it fester.

They sat awhile, hashing the dilemma, getting nowhere. As Blaine left, Teague followed at a distance. Sauntering.

"I'm sorry I can't help you," he told the workman. "I never saw this detail in my face again. I have no special powers or tricks. I can travel in Time, stay forever young. Live well, mostly via theft. But dispose of an infected body? Beyond my ken. And, release her? You'd have to be mad, sir. I was there. I've seen a mass grave."

Two steps down the battered stone, Blaine turned back.

"Excuse this, Teague. I have to ask...what may have been a slip of your tongue..."

Cat stuffed with canary, again.

"About the 'friends'? Is it plural, or just singular?"

Nels Blaine heard his own acknowledgment as dead, dusty. When things got bad in a bar.

"*Yeah....*"

Guy chuckled, open-mouth. He had perfect teeth, better than 1930, better than 2010. Flawless. Real and false, as one.

"That depends," he said, feigning thoughtfulness quite badly, "do *I* count as a person?"

Blaine hated the man. He'd always hated men like this.

"It's exactly what you're thinking, Mr. Blaine," said Guy, withdrawing to doorway. "I do apologize, your having to clean my mess. I'll never apologize for making it."

Old goblet, burnished, cut glass catching the sun. Hoisted, in salute.

"Here's to the Future."

"I guess if you can pretend to be a widower that way, it's a good 'No Fault' divorce."

Thorson's words. It was two hours after sundown. The foreman had met Blaine inside 2001. The situation, fully explained, Blaine had prefaced with words like "dissenters" and "original history". Thorson never peeped, and accepted all he was told. He admitted again, he did not want to do this. Due to the nature of their work, however, it was this simple caper, or a threatening intrigue. No one could know, and everyone would, perhaps even next morning. They had to get Lorna Teague out. Gadgetry could be damaged, marred. Disguised, to a point. The woman had to be spirited off, dead or alive. Nels Blaine insisted she was not only alive, but well.

"The key, is the flu-part," he was saying as they descended the ladder. "A virus, as far as the victim, is internal. Her being is arrested in Time, but that body we see, can't be 100% inert. Not physically. Not and survive. Not for so long."

Thorson stepped to floor.

"And how do you know this?" he asked.

"Same way we're never gonna watch Ted Williams bat against the Mariners."

Using a lax grip on the rails, Blaine slid the last few rungs.

He said, "The science we don't have yet, is 'how d'you preserve alive, with no rotting?' To preserve in our time, freezing is the best we got. For that, you have to kill. Hundreds of years from now, they're able to hit a PAUSE-button. Keep the lifeforce going but suspend it, too."

"So?"

They stood at the wall to the core chamber.

Blaine went on, "Any virus in open air, with just brick around it, mortar, I mean...this core is sealed off, but not for a virus! However lethal it was in 1918, it isn't still active in her system, a hundred years later. It probably wasn't active, a week later! The man's a time traveler. You figure it out."

It didn't take a second. Thorson sighed, leaned into outer foundation brick with one hand.

"'Guess you got sons a' bitches in any era," he said. "I don't know why you'd trouble to leave her alive, walled off."

Blaine shrugged. World weary.

"Same as anyone who doesn't care. They have to have that corn kernel of 'I'm a good person'. The really cold ones, never see the contradiction."

"Shit," Thorson said, low, to the dark brick. "What's the motivation to be that cold?"

"He found something new. As much as said it. They seem to grow 'em much superior, in the 25th Century."

Thorson glared, then straightened, unslinging tools.

"I'll test density, then we can cut ourselves a window."

Not many union minutes later, the men were inside the surreal holy place, humbled, troubled. In someone else's world. They stood before the pale prisoner in grey. Conscious of her curves and soft beauty. Blaine, more involved, was attuned in addition to her pain. A creature from the Great Depression, or an era similar, who couldn't assimilate any other place of being. Marooned, entombed by a man who found he could fly, if he but cut loose his baggage. If Blaine stared at her closed eyelids, it was stamped there, matchbook covers of harm.

Thorson took a seat on the floor, at the base of the chamber-unit. Affected by any sustained close proximity, the unit showed its readout panel. Slowly, like an electric stove heating up. As oversized as the alphabet on a 1st Grade wall, there appeared a touch panel of... Blaine counted a dozen keys, alternating between red and blue in glow, LEDlike, but more a living liquid. Most of the integers were common, listing not 0-9, but 1-10, with 2 odd cyphers at irregular places. The cyphers, simple glyphs, were unknown to the men. Blaine did not understand their presence.

"Anything we do, is guesswork," Thorson reminded him. "It probably won't explode, but you can bet it'll lock us out. I know damned well this'll need some access PIN. If we use 'em, a dictatorship would, forget the year."

"What are those chicken-scratch symbols?" asked Blaine, bending, indicating. "Runes? Some Eastern thing?"

"You see the numerical arrangement," said the foreman. "1 through 6, just as normal, then this jot, like in a retro arcade. Then, 7 through 10, and another 8-bit splotch, and...10, again. I'll sign you over a paycheck, if that second splotch isn't "10", also. Hell of a way they use to keep track."

"So?"

"The system of integers they use in the Future," said Thorson, "is in Base Twelve."

"The Hell is that?"

Thorson sat back, grinning at memories.

"You're too young," he told Blaine. "When I was in the early grades, they tried this idiot thing, supposedly a learning technique. They called it "New Math". It was about understanding what you were doing. Procedure, organization. The way you thought, was the key. Didn't matter, if you got every problem wrong."

Blaine hunkered next to him, scrutinizing the keypad. He was disgusted.

"That's the dumbest thing I ever heard."

Thorson laughed loud at the assessment, forgetting where they were.

"Sure as shit!" he agreed. "They dropped it after a couple years. Just in time for me to learn fractions."

And he laughed again.

"So, what's the number 12 got to do with anything?" Blaine asked.

"No. The New Math pushed the idea of different sets of numbers...could be 1-3, could be 1-8, 1-7...*1-12*, or more. As if you were working it out the everyday 1-10 everybody knows."

Blaine now frowned directly at him.

"What good does that do?"

Thorson replied, "None, I guess, unless you're at CalTech by junior high. But I still know how to do it. The old man was a 'good grades' nut. I had no choice. It's such a fucked up system for thinking, I had to burn it into my brain."

Blaine studied the keys, silent counts through again and again, familiar friends of numbers cut with threatening interlopers. The broader logic made sense at least, future science using alternate calculating methods, adapting to them as society's needs evolved.

"Base Twelve," words as quiet prayer. "Can you still do it in your head?"

"Sure, start me out. She died how long, before he hooked her in?"

"Teague said six or seven hours. Do we guess high or low?"

"Low. Six," said Thorson. "We're working her shelf life in reverse. 60 minutes times 6, is 360. In Base Twelve, it's 72 minutes, which, times 6, would be..."

"Four hundred and thirty-two minutes," said Blaine, greeting Thorson's take with, "*I* can do that much."

"Yeah. And I'll say you're right about the flu-part. No way hundreds of years from now, they can travel in time and space, but not know viruses have a half life. A dude from the Past, though..."

"Whether he knew to start or not, Teague hooked her into the chamber, backed her into life, then left her walled here, for close to a century. If he didn't know, he never asked? Does it matter what year he washed his hands?"

"That's grim philosophy," said the foreman, as they stared up from their position at the pale matron, innocent prisoner of Long Ago.

"That's grim reality," said Blaine. "So, 4-3-2? It can only fail."

"Or lock us out," reminded Thorson. "Any science they're using in four centuries, has to be exact. You have a new kind of person, by then."

Blaine agreed, finishing the thought. "They'd know exactly. They wouldn't estimate. Teague knew it was either/or, which one. What a shitheel."

"What about stray minutes?"

"Not this man," Blaine scoffed. "He lives all-Future, but he's from the Past. For handy memory, you keep it simple. If anyone got close, it's another way to keep them out."

"Do-gooders," said Thorson. "Those meddling kids!"

"And we are," said Blaine, restraining himself from furthering the joke. "4, then 3, then 2. Looks like a Self Enter. Just the three keys."

Thorson glanced again, making eye contact. They were boys sunk into a risky prank. Still not motivated to follow through, the foreman regardless leaned forward from sitting, and depressed the necessary keys.

At the first sounds from the unit, Nels Blaine looked up, yearning. Hoping, as to behold the sun.

Guy Teague stepped into the tall shower stall. His shadow jumped as his lover adjusted bathroom lighting. With a gasping laugh, she was in with him before the water, the hottest the cheap cabin could give, was running full.

The woman, Trae-E'lyn, once a propulsion clinician in the 25th Century, currently an Enemy of the State, found sex as funny as it was pleasurable. There were other methods for deep connection, in her time. Guy had taught her to love the ancient. *"This is all we are."* Once the scientist had opened her eyes to that, she'd had little use for a stratified society of control and order. Trae-E'lyn had use now only for herself, Guy, and their bond as literal "partners in crime". Anyone and anything else, including wives and their beating hearts, could go screw. So to speak.

She whispered that thought into Guy's ear as he lifted her clear of the floor. He, then turning them and turning them until soaked from forceful spray. The water was picking up more heat, and fog began around them. The close narrowness of the stall was something beautiful, something dear to both. Private prehistory. Reality claimed as personal, outside of Time.

Trae-E'lyn was white-blonde, and lupine of stark, sharp features. Borderline anorexic as measured in this 21st Century, but standard physicality in an era and culture of the chemically nourished. Guy had too taught her the joys of ancient food and sustenance. The tastes were often heavenly, but the more divine, the harder violent nausea rode in its wake. Sex, was much preferable.

Four-limbed stick of large, almond eyes wrapped herself around Guy Teague, accepting the pain of the hot water as pleasurable. The couple, a pair of users and takers, liars and manipulators, had been "friends" for a kind of eternity. After rescuing the condemned Teagues in 1933, Trae-E'lyn had grown too close, too fast to the long-ago man. Research through Nucleic Schematic Archives, provided a natural 'why'.

The Teague's 3 children, subsumed by the Remade Earth, had been farmed to different families and of course, gone on to breed. Half a millennium into the future, Trae-E'lyn was a direct descendent. No moral code existed in 2426, beyond Life For State and State Over Life. Seducing her ancestor, was the clear solution, inevitable. It had been a supreme turn on, and quite easy to accomplish.

They knew no morals now. No truth beyond themselves. Guy and his great-great-greatgreat-greatgreatgreat, made use of Time and the second, stolen unit. They always had money, and always hot for one another. They could have anything they wished, and would never die. Not as long as they stayed in the Past. Somewhere.

They didn't bother with soap or gels, nothing but fiery water. Their world of near walls, was the limitlessness of universes, fantasy through heat vapor. The water, best of hot, hurt, but still felt good. The stall, narrow, close, high-ceilinged, was to the couple, built of steam heat and their heat. Water and sweat. Soup of Dawn bathing the virtually immortal. Scalding consecration for the coldest and most selfish. For Guy and his far, future descendant, there was nothing more godly. In the original verbiage of Man, "perfect" was said "complete". Mating in warm springs of a young world, assisted by technology not achieved but long forgotten. Laughing into each other's mouths, at how far advanced their knowing. This distant family, in self-love. "We", "us", was altar to "I". This was how they liked it, and how they liked one another, lost within mists. Pretending they were in Hell, but everyone else had the place all wrong.

And then the actual Hell of cold air, and moist, sweet vapors escaped, as the shower door swung away.

She was neck to knees in formal funeral dress, pre-1920's as known in the Remade Earth—the garment she had died in. Her hair was caught behind with a black silk ribbon, trimmed in real silver, long since turned. Nels Blaine could not locate her footwear, if she had possessed any for burial, so Lorna stood barefoot upon the white tile. In her hand, a Smith and Atchisson "Percussion". A self-cocking revolver minted in their own 1913, the foot pounds of which had ads promising "clean through!" The wronged wife, trained in girlhood by her father, aimed from the hip.

"Here's what real!" she shouted, harsh, and gave him three and her three, in no particular order.

She lowered her weapon. Her feet were wet upon the foreign white tile of this, another world she did not know. Staring at her dead husband and dead good friend, neither of whom had lived up to their title. Lorna thought about turning around, as she loaded one more bullet into its chamber. Nels, the kind man who'd freed her, had offered to hide her. To teach her. So Lorna might begin, again.

There was one beginning, of course, however they covered it over. Lorna regretted only that she and Guy would be burned and scattered, instead of side by side beneath the earth, in the meadow adjacent to St. Linus, not far from the fall of rocks and the tiny stretch of sand by the ocean. Time, one place, one piece, did in fact never conclude. It was the flesh-human echo of eternity, so one could forget about happy endings, or any endings at all, whatever the world called "true".

Lorna stepped over and around the bodies of those who had offended her, closing the stall door, behind. The hot spray, still running, soaked her hair and her black dress, but this too was consecration. Water in all realities, was life, and life was hers as everlasting.

Scars Publications
http://scars.tv

host of literary magazines *cc&d* and Down in the Dirt
http://scars.tv/ccd, http://scars.tv/dirt

from the Scars site, also visit

http://scars.tv/books

for a full list of books available from Scars Publications,

http://scars.tv/chapbooks

for a full list of chapbooks available from Scars Publications,

http://scars.tv/art

an extensive Scars Publications photography and art collection,

http://scars.tv/sale

for a full list of books available for sale from Scars Publications